New Media Unions

Investigating the wave of unionization that has seen over 60 digital and legacy media outlets unionize since 2015, this book explores how a flash of organizing by digital-first journalists has become a full-blown movement to unionize journalism, particularly in the United States.

Through in-depth interviews with journalists and organizers, *New Media Unions* maps the process of labor organizing, foregrounding journalists' voices and documenting a historic and ongoing moment in the digital media industry. Cohen and de Peuter examine what motivates union drives, then follow journalists through the making of a union from scratch. They explore how journalists strategically self-organize, apply their communication skills to alternative ends, generate affective bonds of solidarity, and build power to confront anti-union campaigns and bargain first contracts, winning significant gains and drafting a new labor code for journalism in a digital age. This book demonstrates that if journalism is to have a future, it must be organized.

New Media Unions provides a counter-perspective on an industry in flux, whose protagonists—young journalists facing precarious futures—are using collective organizing to articulate a bottom-up vision for journalism's future. This is a valuable resource for academics and researchers interested in political economy, journalism studies, and labor studies.

Nicole S. Cohen is an Associate Professor at the University of Toronto. She teaches in the Institute of Communication, Culture, Information and Technology, and in the Faculty of Information. She is the author of *Writers' Rights: Freelance Journalism in a Digital Age* (2016).

Greig de Peuter is an Associate Professor in the Department of Communication Studies at Wilfrid Laurier University. He is the co-author, with Nick Dyer-Witheford, of *Games of Empire: Global Capitalism and Video Games* (2009).

Disruptions: Studies in Digital Journalism
Series editor: Bob Franklin

Disruptions refers to the radical changes provoked by the affordances of digital technologies that occur at a pace and on a scale that disrupts settled understandings and traditional ways of creating value, interacting and communicating both socially and professionally. The consequences for digital journalism involve far reaching changes to business models, professional practices, roles, ethics, products and even challenges to the accepted definitions and understandings of journalism. For Digital Journalism Studies, the field of academic inquiry which explores and examines digital journalism, disruption results in paradigmatic and tectonic shifts in scholarly concerns. It prompts reconsideration of research methods, theoretical analyses and responses (oppositional and consensual) to such changes, which have been described as being akin to 'a moment of mind-blowing uncertainty'.

Routledge's new book series, *Disruptions: Studies in Digital Journalism*, seeks to capture, examine and analyse these moments of exciting and explosive professional and scholarly innovation which characterize developments in the day-to-day practice of journalism in an age of digital media, and which are articulated in the newly emerging academic discipline of Digital Journalism Studies.

Hacking Gender and Technology in Journalism
Sara De Vuyst

New Media Unions
Organizing Digital Journalists
Nicole S. Cohen and Greig de Peuter

User Comments and Moderation in Digital Journalism
Thomas B. Ksiazek and Nina Springer

For more information, please visit: www.routledge.com/Disruptions/book-series/DISRUPTDIGJOUR

New Media Unions
Organizing Digital Journalists

**Nicole S. Cohen and
Greig de Peuter**

Routledge
Taylor & Francis Group

LONDON AND NEW YORK

First published 2020
byRoutledge
4 Park Square, Milton Park, Abingdon, Oxon OX14 4RN

and by Routledge
605 Third Avenue, New York, NY 10017

First issued in paperback 2022

Routledge is an imprint of the Taylor & Francis Group, an informa business

© 2020 Nicole S. Cohen and Greig de Peuter

The right of Nicole S. Cohen and Greig de Peuter to be identified as authors
of this work has been asserted by them in accordance with sections 77 and
78 of the Copyright, Designs and Patents Act 1988.

Publisher's Note
The publisher has gone to great lengths to ensure the quality of this reprint but
points out that some imperfections in the original copies may be apparent.

British Library Cataloguing-in-Publication Data
A catalogue record for this book is available from the British Library

Library of Congress Cataloging-in-Publication Data
A catalog record for this book has been requested

ISBN 13: 978-1-03-247470-0 (pbk)
ISBN 13: 978-1-138-32711-5 (hbk)
ISBN 13: 978-0-429-44945-1 (ebk)

DOI: 10.4324/9780429449451

Typeset in Times New Roman
by Apex CoVantage, LLC

Contents

Acknowledgments

Our first thanks go to the many journalists, union organizers, and union staff who we interviewed for being so generous with their time and for sharing their organizing experiences with us. Their insights, encouragement, and research leads were vital to the completion of this book. We are also grateful to several people for feedback on our proposal and for being our first readers: Enda Brophy, Nick Dyer-Witheford, Megan McRobert, Tanner Mirrlees, Haley Mlotek, Penny O'Donnell, Johanna Weststar, and Tannara Yelland. We thank Dugan Nichols, Madison Trusolino, and Christopher Young for indispensable research assistance. Research funding for this project was provided by the Social Sciences and Humanities Research Council of Canada. Series editor Bob Franklin championed this project from the outset, and we are grateful for his support. Thanks also to Priscille Biehlmann and Jennifer Vennall at Routledge. Finally, we thank our families for their care and support as we researched and wrote this book.

Successful union drives and union affiliation, May 2015–November 2019

This list indicates the names of media outlets or companies where journalists ran successful union drives and the parent unions with which they affiliated. Several outlets named in the list have been shut down, acquired, merged, or sold, so some of these outlet names have changed or combined since unionizing.

	Outlet	Union affiliation
1.	Al-Jazeera America digital	The NewsGuild of New York
2.	Arizona Republic	The NewsGuild-CWA
3.	Ars Technica	The NewsGuild of New York
4.	BuzzFeed News	The NewsGuild of New York
5.	BuzzFeed Canada	Canadian Media Guild/CWA-Canada
6.	CBSN News live streaming channel	Writers Guild of America, East
7.	Chesapeake News Guild (Capital Gazette, Carroll County Times, The Baltimore Sun Media Group)	Washington-Baltimore NewsGuild
8.	Chicago Tribune	Chicago News Guild (The NewsGuild-CWA)
9.	The Columbian	Pacific Northwest Newspaper Guild (The NewsGuild-CWA)
10.	Crosscut and KCTS9	The NewsGuild-CWA
11.	The Daily Progress	The Blue Ridge NewsGuild (Washington-Baltimore NewsGuild/CWA)
12.	DNAinfo and Gothamist	Writers Guild of America, East
13.	The Dodo	Writers Guild of America, East
14.	Fast Company	Writers Guild of America, East
15.	The Florida Times-Union	The NewsGuild-CWA
16.	Fortune (digital staff joined unionized print staff)	The NewsGuild-CWA
17.	Fusion	Writers Guild of America, East

(*Continued*)

(Continued)

	Outlet	Union affiliation
18.	Future Media (GamesRadar+, Guitar Player, Guitar World, Laptop Mag, Live Science, Newsarama, PC Gamer, Space. com, TechRadar, Tom's Guide, and Tom's Hardware)	Writers Guild of America, East
19.	Gawker Media	Writers Guild of America, East
20.	Gimlet Media	Writers Guild of America, East
21.	The Guardian US	The NewsGuild of New York
22.	The Hartford Courant	The NewsGuild-CWA
23.	Huffington Post US	Writers Guild of America, East
24.	Jacobin	The NewsGuild of New York
25.	The Intercept	Writers Guild of America, East
26.	Law360	The NewsGuild of New York
27.	The Los Angeles Times	Media Guild of the West (The NewsGuild-CWA)
28.	Mic.com	The NewsGuild of New York
29.	Missoula Independent	The NewsGuild-CWA
30.	The Morning Call	The NewsGuild-CWA
31.	MTV News	Writers Guild of America, East
32.	The New Republic	The NewsGuild of New York
33.	New York Magazine	The NewsGuild of New York
34.	The New Yorker	The NewsGuild of New York
35.	Omaha World-Herald	The NewsGuild-CWA
36.	Onion Inc. (The Onion, The A.V. Club, ClickHole, The Takeout, Onion Labs, and Onion Inc.'s art, video, and marketing departments)	Writers Guild of America, East
37.	Pioneer Valley NewsGuild (Daily Hampshire Gazette and the Valley Advocate)	The NewsGuild-CWA
38.	Pitchfork Media	The NewsGuild of New York
39.	Quartz	The NewsGuild of New York
40.	Raw Story	Washington-Baltimore NewsGuild
41.	The Real News Network	Washington-Baltimore NewsGuild
42.	Refinery29	Writers Guild of America, East
43.	Rewire.News	Washington-Baltimore NewsGuild
44.	The Ringer	Writers Guild of America, East
45.	The Root	Writers Guild of America, East
46.	Salon	Writers Guild of America, East
47.	Slate	Writers Guild of America, East
48.	The Southern Illinoisan	United Media Guild (The NewsGuild-CWA)
49.	StoryCorps	Communication Workers of America Local 1180

	Outlet	Union affiliation
50.	Talking Points Memo	Writers Guild of America, East
51.	The American Prospect	Washington-Baltimore NewsGuild
52.	ThinkProgress	Writers Guild of America, East
53.	Thrillist	Writers Guild of America, East
54.	Tidewater Media Guild (The Virginian-Pilot, the Daily Press, Virginia Gazette, and Tidewater Review)	NewsGuild-CWA
55.	TIME For Kids (staff join unionized TIME staff)	The NewsGuild of New York
56.	TIME Magazine (digital staff join unionized print staff)	The NewsGuild of New York
57.	Vice Canada	Canadian Media Guild
58.	Vice US	Writers Guild of America, East and Motion Pictures Editors Guild, depending on workers' role
59.	Vice UK	National Union of Journalists
60.	Vox Media	Writers Guild of America, East
61.	WHYY-FM	SAG-AFTRA
62.	Wirecutter	The NewsGuild of New York
63.	Ziff Davis Creators Guild (PCMag, Geek, Mashable, AskMen)	The NewsGuild of New York

Introduction

A positive precedent

It's a smile befitting the making of media labor history. On October 16, 2019, the *Los Angeles Times* published a photo of journalists and bargaining committee co-chairs Caroline A. Miranda and Anthony Pesce high-fiving each other, a beaming smile on Miranda's face. Moments earlier, a tentative agreement was reached between the L.A. Times Guild and the *Los Angeles Times*.[1] The bargaining committee had been in drawn-out first contract negotiations for 15 months, and Guild members mounted several high-profile actions, including sit-ins, walkouts, and social media campaigns, to win a strong contract. And win they did. The proposed agreement contains immediate pay raises (some members will see an $11,000 boost in year one of the three-year contract); limitations on management's ability to outsource work; provisions to increase newsroom diversity (for open positions, managers will have to interview at least two candidates from historically underrepresented groups, including women, Black, Latino, Asian American, Native, and LGBTQ journalists); healthcare benefits; extended parental leave; a just-cause clause (meaning employees can no longer be fired at will); and improved intellectual property rights.[2] When ratified, this will be the first union contract in the "138-year history" of the "steadfastly" non-union paper, and it will transform working conditions for the 475 media workers who belong to the union.[3]

The L.A. Times Guild is one of over 60 new media unions that have formed since Spring 2015. What began as a "wave" of digital-first newsrooms organizing unions has developed into a full-blown movement to unionize journalism in the United States. Although journalism in North America has been a relatively unionized industry since The Newspaper Guild formed in 1933,[4] newspaper union membership has declined over the past few decades alongside shrinking employment in journalism,[5] and until the wave kicked off, unions had not made headway into the expanding digital-first journalism sector. (A few digital outlets were unionized prior to 2015: the Times Company Digital was the first "stand-alone on-line news organization" in the United States to organize in 1995 with The Newspaper Guild of New York, now the NewsGuild of New York;[6] AOL UK unionized with the National Union of Journalists in 2006; progressive news website Truthout in 2009; and The Daily Beast became a unionized shop in 2011 after a merger with *Newsweek*, and negotiated its own collective agreement in 2014. In 2015, Canoe.ca became the first digital site in Canada to unionize.) So, the announcement in April 2015 that Gawker Media was unionizing with the Writers Guild of America, East (WGAE) took the industry and labor movement observers by surprise.

A union, understood by many as a relic of a fading industrial age, belied assumptions about digital-first newsrooms like Gawker: laid-back workplaces staffed by young writers who are underpaid but happy to be employed, fueled by a techno-libertarian ethos more common to tech startups than to legacy media outlets, housed in offices that look more like nightclubs than newsrooms. Indeed, just three months prior to Gawker unionizing, *The Washington Post*'s conclusive account of "why internet journalists don't organize" cited structural and ideological barriers, including limited awareness of unions and no class power among a "generation of younger workers . . . who've built personal brands that they can transfer to other media companies."[7]

Gawker Media's union drive was the first in recent years to challenge assumptions about noncommittal millennial media workers predisposed to job hopping. In a statement announcing unionization, instigator Hamilton Nolan wrote, "the online media industry makes real money. It's now possible to find a career in this industry, rather than just a fleeting job."[8] He argued that journalists need a voice in decisions about their work and working conditions, and listed a few of the major issues that later union drives would thrust into the spotlight: intense working conditions, long hours, unpaid overtime, precarious employment, management disorganization, no benefits, sexual harassment, challenges to editorial independence, and low and wildly unequal pay, especially among women and racialized workers. Nolan indicated broader aspirations, too: "There are plenty of companies in this industry whose workers could desperately use the help of a union. If we can show that it's possible, I hope that a positive precedent will be set."

A precedent was indeed set: soon, journalists at dozens of digital outlets, newspapers, and magazines unionized, including Vice, Huffington Post, Slate, Vox.com, *The New Yorker*, *The Chicago Tribune*, and *New York* magazine. In November 2019, the print and digital editorial, video, design, photo, and social media staffs at 24 publications owned by publishing giant Hearst Communications—including *Cosmopolitan*, *Men's Health*, and *Harper's Bazaar*—announced they were unionizing with the WGAE. If recognized, these 500-plus workers will constitute "one of the largest editorial units in the media industry."[9] By the time we finished writing this book, over 60 outlets had unionized (our list, updated at the time of writing, is on page vii). Workers joined the WGAE, which historically represents film, television, and radio writers, and branches of The NewsGuild, the journalists' wing of the 700,000-member Communication Workers of America. Four years after Nolan's call to arms, what media commentators have called a "wave" of organizing looks more like a movement.

This book investigates a brief but intense period of union organizing in journalism, primarily but not exclusively in digital journalism. Although it has been the digital-first outlets that have attracted most media attention, many newspapers, especially small newspapers, and several magazines have also unionized in recent years. We begin the book by considering the reasons why journalists want to unionize, and follow journalists as they collectively diagnose systemic issues; engage in the process of organizing a union from scratch; face anti-union backlash from management; use communication strategically to mobilize support and win recognition; and participate in collective bargaining, winning significant gains and creating a new labor code for journalism in a digital age. Contemporary unionization in journalism represents continuity through change rather than disruption and novelty. While some elements of organizing campaigns are new and specific to the current dynamics of journalism, many aspects reflect historical patterns of collective organizing and management responses, both within and beyond journalism.

Each chapter considers the range of processes and practices involved in organizing labor unions. Taken together, the insights in this book suggest that if journalism is to have a future, it must be organized. As the journalists who we interviewed have demonstrated, labor organizing is not just about improving working conditions for individuals, but is a broader effort to build organizational infrastructure that can transform journalism, making it accessible, inclusive, and kinder to those whose commitment to journalistic ideals keeps them in such a volatile, precarious industry. Unionization is just one strategy to address journalism's hyper-commodification in contemporary capitalism—others have advocated for public, non-profit journalism and worker-owned co-operatives, for example.[10] Our study of class relations in digital journalism provides a counter-perspective on an industry in flux, whose protagonists—young journalists confronting precarious futures—are using the collective organizing process to articulate a bottom-up vision for journalism's future. As a journalist who helped organize her newsroom told us, "our generation is kind of screwed. And it's going to take unionization to really save us . . . from this precarious situation that we're in."

Journalism, labor, and organizing

The term crisis has been used by scholars and commentators to describe journalism's current state for well over a decade now. At its most narrow, "crisis" is shorthand for the declining profits newspaper corporations enjoy as advertising revenue shifts from print-based to digital media. But the resulting challenges for journalism include mass layoffs of reporters; shuttering of newspapers, especially local and community papers, across Canada and the United States; increased consolidation and concentration; control by and influence of tech giants Facebook and Google; shrinking newsrooms and a corresponding decline in robust reporting; and general uncertainty as for-profit media rapidly adjust business models and strategies in reaction to digital technologies and a changing political economic climate.[11] Such challenges have serious implications for citizens and for journalists, who bear the brunt of change and uncertainty, as crisis discourse is regularly used to justify layoffs, precarious employment, and shrinking journalistic resources.

While not denying that this period of change and uncertainty has serious consequences for journalism, in this book we advocate a shift in perspective from a crisis discourse, which can limit options for change and usually argues for restoring journalism's profitability without questioning its economic organization.[12] Drawing on critical political economy and labor studies perspectives, we propose a focus on collective organizing in journalism as a way to understand its current dynamics. Attending to labor and resistance foregrounds the power and social relations coursing through contemporary journalism—many of which have long been present, such as the challenges of commodifying a social good such as journalism and the class relations between capital and labor—highlighting who pays for journalism's crisis, and who has visions for alternate futures.

While not a major focus of journalism studies and certainly a neglected area of digital journalism scholarship, research on work and labor in journalism has shed light on journalists' working conditions, including speeded-up and intensified workloads, declining autonomy, and precarious work.[13] As one writer puts it, digital media in particular "rclie[s] on its young . . . staff to churn out content, respond nimbly to every change in the Facebook algorithm and sometimes even mine their personal pain for clicks in the pursuit of blistering traffic growth."[14] Scholars have documented journalism history from a labor perspective,[15] and examined the formation of journalists' unions and labor conflict.[16] More recent case studies provide insight and commentary on efforts to unionize journalists in digital and legacy media.[17] This book contributes to this scholarship with an in-depth, empirical study of journalists' efforts to unionize since 2015.

We focus on the process and social relations of organizing. Drawing on labor movement scholars, we conceptualize union organizing as more than an effort to set up an organization to represent journalists, or what may be considered "a set of practices and tactics," as Melanie Simms and Jane Holgate put it. Rather, argue Simms and Holgate, organizing should be considered a "wider political initiative" that privileges "worker self-organization for power."[18] The aim of organizing should not just be membership growth for the sake of it, but rather building worker power with political objectives in mind.[19] Such an approach is evident among the new media unions forming in journalism. As we demonstrate, while parent unions play key roles in organizing unions, self-organization is a vital dynamic propelling the new media union movement, and journalists' aims coalesce around democratizing the workplace, fairness, equity, and safeguarding their ability to practice journalism with integrity.

Key to organizing, stress Simms and Holgate, is to ask what unions are organizing for. For Jane McAlevey, organizing's "primary purpose is to change the power structure."[20] Organizing is not just about improving material gain for union members, although certainly improvements to pay and benefits are core motivators. More so, organizing is aimed at empowering "ordinary" people, as McAlevey puts it, to develop a power analysis that can be used for long-term transformation. As the following chapters demonstrate, the unionizing process has enabled journalists to develop and deepen a power analysis of the industry in which they work and the relations between those who hold powerful positions—management, owners, and media companies—and those who do the labor of producing the journalism that keeps companies going. Organizing helps workers "connect the dots" between their individual experiences and "the larger system" in which they live and work, and, ultimately, aims to "transfer power from the elite to the majority."[21] Through organizing, journalists have articulated a vision of sustainability, accessibility, equity, and integrity, core expectations that can improve individual working conditions while raising standards across the industry and ensuring journalistic work is accessible and protected.

As Astra Taylor writes, organizing "aims to bring others into the fold, to build and exercise shared power," and "involves . . . aggregating people around common interests so that they can strategically wield their combined strength."[22] The work of organizing, she adds, is threefold. It requires "creating infrastructure and institutions, finding points of vulnerability and leverage in the situation you want to transform, and convincing atomized individuals to recognize that they are on the same team (and to behave like it)." Prior to 2015, as Lydia DePillis highlighted in the *Washington Post*, digital journalists were understood to be brand-building, competitive individuals hustling to secure coveted positions at hyped media companies, whatever the cost (usually low salaries and burnout). But studying efforts to unionize digital journalism, and journalism more broadly, shows that young media workers are just as inclined to build and mobilize solidarity and friendships, as they realize it's employers who benefit most from journalists estimating their value in individualized terms. As sociologist Rick Fantasia writes, "in a society in which individual initiative is held to be the only legitimate avenue of social mobility and improvement, collective action is a remarkable accomplishment."[23]

Digital journalists organize

The entrance of more than 2,000 young media workers into the labor movement in five short years is remarkable indeed. To understand this development, we conducted 49 in-depth interviews with 48 people (some were group interviews, and some follow-up interviews) between October 2016 and July 2019. We interviewed journalists who served on organizing committees or bargaining committees in 20 different newsrooms, as well as union staff at the WGAE and the Canadian Media Guild, The NewsGuild, The NewsGuild of New York, and the Washington-Baltimore NewsGuild. While we identify some participants in the book, most have chosen to remain anonymous. We also draw on media coverage, observation of union social media accounts, union-produced documents, and collective bargaining agreements. The story we tell in the following pages is shaped by the perspective of those we interviewed, who all were either active organizers and leaders in their unions or union staff and organizers. While we critically assess the limits and possibilities of the movement to unionize journalism, overall, we share our interviewees' perspective that transforming digital journalists' material conditions through collective organizing is vital for ensuring journalism as a form of potentially democratic communications has a sustainable future in the digital age.

A note on terminology: throughout the book, we use the term journalist because we are mostly writing about workers who do journalistic work, or who "research, investigate, interpret and communicate news and public affairs" in newspapers and digital formats.[24] Despite this general description, we recognize that journalistic work is transforming and that people perform a great diversity of work in both digital and print-based outlets—new bargaining units include social media editors, photographers, and video producers, for example. Therefore, we also use the term media worker throughout the book, which enables an expansive understanding of the ever-changing terrain of media production, where the divide between "legacy" and digital media is increasingly blurred.

The book's organization follows the process of organizing, or the steps involved in moving from considering the idea of a union to bargaining a first collective agreement, highlighting the social relations that make collective action possible and powerful. Chapter 1, "Motivation," examines what compels digital media workers to form unions, including improving working conditions, gaining a voice, safeguarding editorial integrity, addressing racial and gender inequity, protecting workers during layoffs, and confronting industry volatility. Chapter 2, "Activation," outlines the forces that propel a collective diagnosis of problems into full-fledged union drives, and the broader contextual and structural conditions that have made digital media worker unionization possible. Chapter 3, "Mobilization," looks in detail at how organizing drives unfold, paying particular attention to the affective modes journalists have embraced in digital media union drives and the central role communication has played in organizing. Chapter 4, "Recognition," focuses on the struggle unions have faced to win recognition—including aggressive management anti-union campaigns—and how workers mount strategic public pressure campaigns that also serve to build solidarity in and between newsrooms. Chapter 5, "Negotiation," explains the process of collectively bargaining a first contract and assesses the first collective bargaining agreements that have so far been won, many of which include important gains for the sector that have raised journalists' salaries, provided a modicum of stability, and boosted expectations overall. Chapter 6, "Transformation," considers how journalists, newsrooms, and unions have been transformed through the organizing surge in digital media.

In addition to a piece of scholarly research and a public document of a particular moment in journalism and labor movement history, we hope this book will also serve as a guide for other workers seeking to organize their workplaces. If we can leave readers with one point, it's one made by a journalist who started a union in her digital newsroom: "if you don't have a union," she says, "you can make one."[25]

Notes

1   Meg James, "Los Angeles Times Reaches Historic Agreement with Its Newsroom," *Los Angeles Times*, October 16, 2019, www.latimes.com/california/story/2019-10-16/los-angeles-times-first-guild-contract.

2   L.A. Times Guild, "L.A. Times Guild Reaches Agreement with Management on Historic First Contract," *LA Times Guild*, October 16, 2019, https://latguild.com/news/2019/10/16/los-angeles-times-guild-reaches-agreement.

3   James, "Los Angeles Times Reaches Historic Agreement with Its Newsroom."

4   Daniel J. Leab, *A Union of Individuals: The Formation of the American Newspaper Guild, 1933–1936* (New York: Columbia University Press, 1970).

5   Elizabeth Grieco, "Newsroom Employment Dropped Nearly a Quarter in Less Than 10 Years, with Greatest Decline at Newspapers," *Pew Research Center*,

July 30, 2018, www.pewresearch.org/fact-tank/2018/07/30/newsroom-employ
ment-dropped-nearly-a-quarter-in-less-than-10-years-with-greatest-decline-at-
newspapers/.

6 Errol Salamon, "Digital Media Workers are Unionizing Like It's 1999,"
Rankandfile.ca, April 5, 2016, http://rankandfile.ca/digital-media-workers-are-
unionizing-like-its-1999/.

7 Lydia DePillis, "Why Internet Journalists Don't Organize," *The Washington Post*,
January 30, 2015, www.washingtonpost.com/news/storyline/wp/2015/01/30/
why-internet-journalists-dont-organize/.

8 Hamilton Nolan, "Why We've Decided to Organize," *Gawker*, April 16, 2015,
http://gawker.com/why-weve-decided-to-organize-1698246231.

9 Maxwell Tani, "Hearst Magazine Staffers Unionizing Across Two Dozen Publications, Forming Giant for Writers Guild of America," *The Daily Beast*, November
11, 2019, www.thedailybeast.com/hearst-magazines-staffers-are-unionizing-
across-two-dozen-publications-joining-writers-guild-of-america-east.

10 Victor Pickard, "The Violence of the Market," *Journalism* 20, no. 1 (2019):
154–8; Kim Kelly, "Seize the Media," *Commune*, May 2, 2019, https://com
munemag.com/seize-the-media/.

11 Jeffrey C. Alexander, Elizabeth Butler Breese, and María Leungo, eds., *The
Crisis of Journalism Reconsidered: Democratic Culture, Professional Codes,
Digital Future* (New York: Cambridge University Press, 2016); Robert W.
McChesney and Victor Pickard, eds., *Will the Last Reporter Please Turn Out
the Lights: The Collapse of Journalism and What Can Be Done to Fix It* (New
York: The New Press, 2011); Mike Gasher, Colette Brin, Christine Crowther,
Gretchen King, Errol Salamon, and Simon Thibault, eds., *Journalism in Cri-
sis: Bridging Theory and Practice for Democratic Media Strategies in Canada*
(Toronto: University of Toronto Press, 2016); Emily Bell and Taylor Owen, *The
Platform Press: How Silicon Valley Reengineered Journalism*, Tow Center for
Digital Journalism, Columbia University, March 2017, www.cjr.org/tow_center_
reports/platform-press-how-silicon-valley-reengineered-journalism.php.

12 See Pickard, "The Violence of the Market."

13 See, for example: Nicole S. Cohen, *Writers' Rights: Freelance Journalism in a
Digital Age* (Montreal and Kingston: McGill-Queen's University Press, 2016);
Nicole S. Cohen, "At Work in the Digital Newsroom," *Digital Journalism* 7, no.
5 (2019): 571–91; Caitlin Petre, "Engineering Consent: How the Design and Mar-
keting of Newsroom Analytics Tools Rationalized Journalists' Labor," *Digital
Journalism* 6, no. 4 (2018): 509–27; Errol Salamon, "Digitizing Freelance Media
Labor: A Class of Workers Negotiates Entrepreneurialism and Activism," *New
Media & Society*, July 17, 2019, https://doi.org/10.1177/1461444819861958;
Merryn Sherwood and Penny O'Donnell, "Once a Journalist, Always a Journalist?
Industry Restructure, Job Loss and Professional Identity," *Journalism Studies* 19,
no. 7 (2016): 1021–38; Sasu Siegelbaum and Ryan J. Thomas, "Putting the Work
(Back) into Newswork: Searching for the Sources of Normative Failure," *Journal-
ism Practice* 10, no. 3 (2016): 387–404; James R. Compton and Paul Benedetti,
"Labour, New Media, and the Institutional Restructuring of Journalism," *Jour-
nalism Studies* 11, no. 4 (2010): 487–99; Henrik Örnebring, "Technology and
Journalism-as-Labour: Historical Perspectives," *Journalism* 11, no. 1 (2010): 57–74.

14 Maxwell Strachan, "The Fall of Mic Was a Warning," *HuffPost US*, July 23, 2019,
www.huffingtonpost.ca/entry/mic-layoffs-millennial-digital-news-site-warning_
n_5c8c144fe4b03e83bdc0e0bc.

15 Hanno Hardt and Bonnie Brennen, eds., *Newsworkers: Toward a History of the Rank and File* (Minneapolis: University of Minnesota Press, 1995).

16 Leab, *A Union of Individuals*; Walter M. Brasch, *With Just Cause: Unionization of the American Journalist* (Lanham: University Press of America, 1991); Catherine McKercher, *Newsworkers Unite: Labor, Convergence, and North American Newspapers* (Lanham: Rowman & Littlefield, 2002); Chris Rhomberg, *The Broken Table: The Detroit Newspaper Strike and the State of American Labor* (New York: Russell Sage Foundation, 2012).

17 Tai Neilson, "Unions in Digital Labour Studies: A Review of Information Society and Marxist Autonomist Approaches," *tripleC* 16, no. 2 (2018): 882–900; Richard Wells, "Connecting the Dots: Labor and the Digital Landscape," *Labor Studies in Working-Class History* 15, no. 3 (2018): 55–76; Nicole Cohen and Greig de Peuter, "Write, Post, Unionize: Journalists and Self-Organization," *Notes from Below*, June 8, 2019, https://notesfrombelow.org/article/write-post-unionize; Nicole Cohen and Greig de Peuter, "'I Work at VICE Canada and I Need a Union': Organizing Digital Media," in *Labour under Attack: Anti-Unionism in Canada*, eds. Stephanie Ross and Larry Savage (Halifax and Winnipeg: Fernwood, 2018), 114–28; Revati Prasad, "An Organized Workforce Is Part of Growing Up: Gawker and the Case for Unionizing Digital Newsrooms," *Communication, Culture & Critique*, March 2019, https://doi.org/10.1093/ccc/tcz008; Jennifer M. Proffitt, "Solidarity in the Newsroom? Media Concentration and Union Organizing: A Case Study from the Sunshine State," *Journalism*, June 2019, https://doi.org/10.1177/1464884919860030.

18 Melanie Simms and Jane Holgate, "Organising for What? Where Is the Debate on the Politics of Organising?," *Work, Employment & Society* 24, no. 1 (2010): 157–68, 158.

19 Simms and Holgate, "Organising for What?," 161.

20 Jane McAlevey, *No Shortcuts: Organizing for Power in the New Gilded Age* (Oxford: Oxford University Press, 2016), 12.

21 McAlevey, *No Shortcuts*, 201, 10.

22 Astra Taylor, "Against Activism," *The Baffler*, no. 30 (2016), https://thebaffler.com/salvos/against-activism.

23 Rick Fantasia, *Cultures of Solidarity: Consciousness, Action, and Contemporary American Workers* (Berkeley: University of California Press, 1988), 132.

24 Statistics Canada, "5123—Journalists," National Occupational Classification 2011, 2018, accessed October 16, 2019, http://www23.statcan.gc.ca/imdb/p3VD.pl?Function=getVD&TVD=122372&CVD=122376&CPV=5123&CST=01012011&CLV=4&MLV=4.

25 Tannara Yelland, presentation at "Remaking Game Work," public forum, Toronto Media Arts Centre, July 17, 2019.

1 Motivation

Insidery

On April 16, 2015, less than 24 hours after a preliminary meeting at the Writers Guild of America, East (WGAE) office, Gawker Media journalists announced their union bid with gusto online via a Gawker post titled "Why We've Decided to Organize."[1] Going so public so fast made WGAE organizers uneasy. The publicity defied typical union drive strategy: keep the effort quiet until you reach critical mass, or your hand is forced. But "radical transparency" was a Gawker credo. In the post, which was tagged "too insidery," journalist Hamilton Nolan outlined reasons for organizing, from making a fair salary to "giving employees a voice." He captured a first principle of organizing: "A union is . . . the only real mechanism that enables employees to join together to bargain collectively, rather than as a bunch of separate, powerless entities." In hindsight, the post was the unofficial announcement of the digital media union movement. The decision to break the news this way reflects journalists' "insidery" insight on how to best spread the word to colleagues at other digital outlets. Yet the idea to report on the drive (and, later, debate publicly how workers were voting on the union) was encouraged by Gawker top brass, who saw a brand-reinforcing opportunity to generate traffic. That Gawker would soon shut down—leveled by a lawsuit bankrolled by a right-wing billionaire, later acquired at a discount by a venture media capitalist—underscores the industry volatility and political climate underpinning the "wave" of organizing in digital media.

What, in this context, drives primarily young digital journalists with little to no experience in the labor movement to organize unions? Theories of collective action shed some light on this question.[2] Collective action tends to emerge amid discontent with the status quo. To eventually prompt workers to take collective action, "dissatisfaction at work" must take the form of a "sense of injustice" or "grievance,"[3] or the feeling that "an event, action, or situation is 'wrong' or 'illegitimate.'"[4] Typically, collective action is motivated by workers identifying with each other and recognizing shared grievances. Rather than disenchantment with an inchoate force, collective action requires that workers attribute a problem to a specific source—not only to pin the "blame" on a particular entity (a boss, for example), but also to figure out how to "remedy" the situation.[5] Determining shared interests is intrinsic to this process of collective identification: "To what extent do [workers] believe their interests to be similar to, different from, or opposed to, those of the ruling group?"[6] The eventual decision to engage in collective action also rests on a belief that workers can win. Writes John Kelly, "It is not enough for employees to feel aggrieved: they must also feel entitled to their demands and feel that there is some chance that their situation can be changed by 'collective agency.'"[7]

The swift unionization at Gawker did inspire other newsrooms to act, but Gawker's unionization doesn't fully account for the movement underway. This chapter is a partial inventory of the motivations and aspirations compelling digital journalists to organize. We find that the reasons for seeking union representation are as varied as the outlets involved; pay, for example, may be a primary motivating factor in one newsroom and not pressing in another. This chapter begins to trace the process of unionization, focusing on the period prior to journalists formally initiating union drives, and gives insight into working conditions in digital media. In the newsrooms we studied, union drives have not just been a reaction to narrow workplace-based frustrations. The journalists we interviewed often frame their motives in terms of transforming journalism in the name of sustainable careers, expanded and equitable access, and editorial integrity. This chapter maps patterns in journalists' sources of frustration, grievances that are frequently articulated as endemic to the digital media industry.

Reckoning

Whether their beat is foreign policy or heavy metal, the journalists we interviewed are clearly devoted to and enjoy their work. One journalist captures the general sentiment: "the work is so valuable and so interesting." Equally clear, however, is that passionate commitment to the work is not enough for journalists to ignore the downsides. "Putting out the same content, day in day out—it's a grind, like any job," one journalist-organizer admits. On balance, the problems that digital journalists face in their work are not entirely unique to either the digital age or to their profession. "These are people who are struggling like everyone else," one editor says. "These are white-collar workers but they're . . . [unionizing] for the same reasons that anybody else would." Digital journalists are organizing to improve the terms and conditions of their employment and to gain increased control over their work and craft. Journalists describe the material conditions and workplace culture in digital newsrooms on a spectrum, ranging from "horrible" to largely decent but needing improvement.

Pay regularly tops journalists' list of grievances. Low salaries were "the biggest issue" at Vice, for example, and "people would go years without raises" at Gothamist, says a writer. Many journalists have a "hard time paying their bills," says the WGAE's executive director, Lowell Peterson, especially considering the cost of living in a city like New York, where jobs are clustered. Digital media companies trade on their carefully cultivated glamorous self-image and appeal to start-up status, and they rely on employees' vocational devotion to justify subpar wages. "The whole underlying, unspoken thing," says one Vice journalist, "is that you're lucky to work here, so shut up and work. Like, Vice is cool. And that's why I think people take the shitty pay or the pay cuts." Journalists are increasingly recognizing employers' strategies for squeezing labor costs: "the industry is long overdue for a reckoning with the you-should-be-so-lucky-to-have-this-job mentality," one journalist says. Post-and-beam offices, the social cachet of digital media brands, "cool swag and . . . a verified Twitter" are all "bread and circuses," says Kim Kelly, who helped organize the Vice union in the United States. But it's not just salary levels that bother journalists—it's also lack of transparency about pay. "Nobody knows what anybody makes. Nobody knows what an 'associate editor' should make [for example]. . . . Nobody has any idea of what they should be making," says a journalist. Lack of transparency is an industry-wide problem. With no benchmark to reference—not to mention the challenge that the same job title can mean quite different things at different media organizations—new hires have little reliable information to support them in initial salary negotiations.

Dissatisfaction with compensation scales to a sense of injustice when journalists recognize that salaries are unfair. While the extent of inequity has not always been grasped until deeper into an organizing drive, journalists have been sharing enough with each other to understand that salaries and benefits are sometimes wildly inconsistent between people performing similar work in their newsroom. Employment terms at Vox were "all individualized," says a journalist. Such discussions prompted questions that seem mundane—"Why did that person get approved to work at home some days of the week and I didn't?" asked a Vice worker—but are, in fact, moral matters. "Fairness," says a union organizer, "is often a reason people choose to organize." She describes a newsroom where journalists "knew their salaries weren't great, but the motivator was knowing that some people were getting paid fine and other people were getting paid many thousands of dollars less, and no one could really figure out why." Stoking the perception of injustice in some workplaces, informal disclosures among colleagues have shown that salary discrepancies are not entirely arbitrary, but based on gender and race, which workers hope unionization can fix.

Journalists have other issues with how workplaces are managed. One journalist describes their pre-unionized newsroom as a "mess, it was just chaos." Workers' problems with management and the severity of those problems vary by outlet. Some journalists were dismayed by inexperienced managers: "our head of content was 27 years old, had never managed anybody before, and now was suddenly in charge," says a Vice Canada journalist.[8] Another says people were annoyed with what seemed like perpetually "shifting goalposts for what you were expected to do." Others still were frustrated that management promises failed to materialize, like a promise at MTV News to convert permalancers (workers hired on so many back-to-back, short-term contracts that they are de facto permanent employees, minus the security and benefits) to full-time status. A former Al Jazeera America journalist explains the slow dissipation of initial "great hope":

> as that sense sets in, it breeds a cynicism, a frustration, a little bit of anger. A year goes by and there are no salary reviews, very few promotions, no raises, some questionable personnel decisions, then a mentality sets in that, shall we say, is . . . ripe for organizing.

Workers' unease often stems from a holdover of start-up culture, informality, which leads to ad hoc workplace regulation. Of Gawker, says Nolan, "stuff wasn't standardized, it was run by how your boss feels." Lackluster communication has been another common complaint. Overall, journalists want to formalize workplace relations, especially at digital-first or new outlets. As one journalist explains, her colleagues needed a "structure that actually forces the ones with more knowledge to inform the ones without it. . . . Otherwise, there was this . . . unintentional inequality . . . this was stuff that was really eating at them." The predominant sense from our interviews was that journalists are motivated to "fix" their workplaces, and expect companies to live up to the ideals they reflect in published content. The attribution of outright malice to management has been rare, largely limited to cases of the perceived unfair dismissal of colleagues.

Job security has been a motivating factor, especially as closures and layoffs picked up in recent years. In some cases, this concern is linked to a specific event, like a dubious firing or impending restructuring, but generally journalists share "a sense of wanting to protect ourselves." Journalists consistently characterize employment insecurity as an industry-wide problem. "Precarity and uncertainty in the industry" is ultimately what's driving digital media union campaigns, says a NewsGuild organizer. Legacy media organizations might have provided, or at least promised, "pretty stable careers" to a previous generation of journalists, she says, but "that's just not the reality for most young digital workers entering into the workforce and having to jump around two or three or four different jobs by the time [they're] 30." Journalists who start in an unpaid internship, graduate to freelancing, become a permalancer, and change employers multiple times in the first years of their careers—all while carrying student debt—are no strangers to precarity.

Even if they do hold an indefinite employment contract, digital journalists are acutely aware that their field is shaky, with business models in flux, ad revenues elusive, and layoffs chronic. "Everybody knows we're all . . . advancing on the lip of a volcano," says a journalist. "There's no way to be safe or secure in this business," says Kelly. "Because you could wake up one day and the billionaire who owns the company could be in jail, or decide to sell, or decide that everyone needs to do video." It's in this context of industry tumult that journalists are demanding a "safety net for people . . . when that stuff happens." But since job hopping is industry standard, voluntarily or otherwise, securing protections at one's current workplace is not a long-term livelihood strategy. Framing unstable employment in industry-wide terms has enabled digital media unionization to become a "movement" for change across the sector, underpinned by a determination of collective interest and energized by a "desire for collective security."[9]

Work intensity has also stoked discontent, including complaints of excessive hours. While some people describe punishing back-to-back workdays interspersed with "some sleeping," most journalists accept crunch as a fact of deadline-driven media work and a profession that puts a premium on immediacy. Dissatisfaction arises when overtime is unpaid, unrecognized, or expected. At some outlets, extreme hours and a "both-ends-burning kind of culture" remain a badge of honor. Such expectations have been an escalating source of grievance not only for workers with children or other caring responsibilities, but for all workers, whose basic need for rest and a life outside of work is neglected by such an ethos. Claims on workers' time regularly extend beyond the spatial bounds of the newsroom to the expectation that journalists be perpetually available, what Melissa Gregg calls "presence bleed."[10] "People are expected to be on call and on email and on their phones all the time," says a journalist-organizer. "So many people feel like they can't ignore it. They feel beholden to their phone."

Digital journalists have been frustrated with productivity expectations generally. "The story quotas were a huge, huge problem," says an organizer. Another says journalists "tweet and write and pitch constantly to stay relevant in an exhausting 24/7/365 media cycle." As with job security, journalists describe the intensification of work as an industry-wide issue: "at their worst, that's what online publications have been: . . . all-consuming beasts that you're constantly trying to feed with content," says a journalist. "No one can work at that pace." Another says that when she tried to express workload-related complaints, her manager would "reframe" the issue in "emotional terms," telling her that her "nerves were frayed," adding a gendered dimension to the culture of overwork in digital newsrooms.

The requirement to monitor data analytics exacerbates stress. As one journalist describes:

> You're watching the traffic. You're watching Chartbeat. . . . You're watching multiple data. You're watching Twitter. You're watching *New York Times, Washington Post* . . . TV channels to try to keep abreast. . . . It's very much a multi-tasking kind of thing. . . . You can't really give your whole self to anything. . . . And you're not made of out of wood, there's an emotional toll.

The human cost of toiling in the hidden abode of producing journalism for fleeting, swipe-through attention economies is starkly captured by a journalist who works remotely. After suffering a heart attack, one of his initial thoughts from his hospital bed was that at least he wouldn't have to work that night. "[The job] is literally killing you at that point," he says, "when it's like, I'd rather be dangling by a thread in ER than work a four-to-midnight shift, another Saturday night, by myself." Such grievances about work intensity have a clear remedy: protected limits. So, while journalists' sources of discontent with their working conditions do have occupation-specific inflections, the desire for "a workload that's more psychologically reasonable" and for a semblance of work-life balance are as universal as the labor justice impulse to, as this journalist puts it, "demand your fucking dignity." As McAlevey reminds us, "scholars assume that material gain is the primary concern of unions, missing that workplace fights are most importantly about one of the deepest of human emotional needs: dignity."[11]

The voice option

The media workers who have initiated union drives aspire to raise standards in digital journalism. They are pushing back against attitudes that devalue online writing. "We've been made to feel like we . . . just blog and click-bait and turn out words that are going to disappear tomorrow," says Kelly. "We have been made to feel that our work is ephemeral. . . . But it's not, because the internet ain't going nowhere." Even so, new entrants' expectations of the industry are marked by layoffs-fueled coverage of journalism's financial crisis. "People are basically coming into this knowing on the front end that these jobs are not going to be sustainable," says an organizer. Still, despite industry tumult, not all digital journalists want to exit journalism even if, as another organizer says, "They see their colleagues leave for PR firms, because it pays better and is more secure, and wonder if they should do the same." Rather, a commitment to their work and a desire to improve conditions has led them to opt for what economist Albert Hirschman calls "the voice option," which is "the only way in which dissatisfied . . . members can react whenever the exit option is unavailable."[12] "Voice," writes Hirschman, is "any attempt at all to change, rather than to escape from, an objectionable state of affairs."[13]

Unionizing is a way for journalists to resist the precarious status quo. Many want "the basic ability to do this job that we think is important to society," as one writer puts it. A journalist laments, "a production assistant making $30,000 a year—in New York City—that doesn't work for anybody." Beyond raising salary floors, healthcare has been a "prime motivator" for some workers to seriously consider organizing their newsrooms. Digital media workers hold these "prominent, high-status positions," while their employers "[hope] that they'll never write about the fact that they don't have healthcare," says an editor. In time, she says, "they'll start getting really mad . . . feeling that they deserve better." The journalists we interviewed also believe that they deserve better in everyday workplace relations, ranging from protections against harassment to being in what one describes as an "environment where you don't necessarily feel . . . you've gotta turn up for work when there are . . . other important demands, human demands, on you." Acknowledging the existence of needs that cannot be satisfied by a byline, journalist-organizers want to make digital media careers more sustainable.

A main grievance driving collective action in digital newsrooms has been what one journalist describes as "the homogeneity of our industry." To be sure, there are outlier cases. More than half of Fusion's staff, we are told, are Latinx, and The Root is staffed by journalists of color, for example. But the exceptions prove the rule. An organizer who has an inside view of dozens of US newsrooms says, "It's a very white industry." At many outlets, journalists are frustrated by the lack of racial diversity in their newsrooms, classifying their workplaces on a narrow spectrum, from "pretty white" to "mostly white" to "overwhelmingly white." "When it came to racial diversity," says one journalist-organizer, "we definitely had a problem." Of the New York City-focused publication for which this journalist worked, she adds, it "did not feel like a representative cross-section of New York City." Other journalists, says an organizer, have been agitated by the gap between media discourse and media employment: "We're constantly talking about structural racism, but our newsrooms are always looking exactly the same."

Alongside race-based disparities, journalists are disaffected by gender- and class-based inequities in digital media. While journalists characterize several newsrooms as being more or less balanced in terms of women and men journalists, we were unsurprisingly told that leadership or executive positions tend to skew male. As one journalist says of the division of duties in her newsroom: "so much of the labor . . . was being done by women on behalf of men who gave the instructions." Journalists identify gendered power relations in multiple workplace dimensions, from unequal access to career development opportunities to a lingering "bro culture." Journalists are also concerned about the class inequalities marring their profession. One source of discontent is the legacy of unpaid internships, which a journalist describes as a "barrier to entry for anyone but the most economically privileged college students." Others point out that digital journalism's low salaries are less of a burden for those who can count on family subsidy. Inequities in who gets to pursue media careers reflect "the class warfare that's gone on for years and . . . made journalism less and less accessible to people who aren't wealthy and don't have trust funds," says a journalist.

Journalists are motivated to widen the social range of voices in digital media. They recognize, as one journalist-organizer puts it, that we "do not represent the society that we are reporting on behalf of." Journalists anticipate that more diverse newsrooms will produce better journalism, and increase the ability to "do stories that we think our audience would want [and] do them more responsibly," says a journalist. Most regard expanded diversity as achievable partly because they've experienced first-hand exposure to the managerial practices through which industry homogeneity is perpetuated. Many flag the informality of recruitment, namely hiring via existing social networks, as replicating social inequalities in the workforce.[14] One journalist describes a default recruitment strategy: "'We have an opening.' 'Oh, I have a buddy, let me send you their resume.'" Another adds, "no one posted my job publically. I got a text message." Such well-known informal hiring practices are, she says, "just part of the white supremacist infrastructure of our culture." Journalists want to disrupt this culture in their workplaces through opening recruitment processes, creating rules around equitable hiring, and introducing simple measures like advertising posts more widely and strategically.

Workers' dissatisfaction with their employers crosses the grievance threshold when the employer appears to violate accepted norms. Journalism's professional principle of autonomy is decisive in this respect. "[E]ditorial freedom from corporate influence is another really big thing that's driving this," says a WGAE organizer. For example, HuffPost journalists wanted to safeguard "editorial independence" from founder Arianna Huffington's interests. Journalists are concerned about the impact of sponsored content on their craft. Some journalists expressed discomfort with being asked by marketing staff to brainstorm on advertiser-driven content, feeling a lack of security to say, "Hey, I think you just casually breached one of the most important rules of our profession," says a Vice journalist-organizer. Writers wanted a "clearer wall" between editorial and advertising in the name of journalistic integrity. Framing their grievance through a professional ethics lens has helped define a collective interest. "Is it okay to get a company to pay for a journalistic product?" asks a journalist-organizer. "And, if it is, what's the dividing line?" Others worry about sponsored content's long-term ramifications for their profession: "[A]re we journalists, or are we not?" Media organizations that rely on the support of the celebrities they cover have posed unique challenges. One journalist was frustrated that there was no transparent or consistent way to respond when a star complained about a post. What she wanted was simply a formal protocol that would involve the writer and would not be determined by, say, "whatever mood [an executive] was in that day."

In union parlance, journalists want to formalize workers' voice on the job. Voice is suppressed in multiple ways in digital newsrooms. Feeling "lucky" to land work in a culturally desirable and intensely competitive industry doesn't foster confidence to speak out. One journalist recounts being told at her job interview that "there were people lining up at the door for my position, we felt that on a daily basis. When you're just starting out and there's a million people who can take your place at any time, it's really scary to negotiate with these people." Journalists are frustrated by their lack of power to formally address the sort of grievances we survey in this chapter. Says one journalist, "you just have no voice as an employee there." Another comments: "we want more of a say in what our work looks like." Journalist-organizers have no illusions that their employers can guarantee a "long-term job, since things do happen"—but they still want "to have some say in that experience." Whether the issue is salary or severance, equitable hiring or editorial process, journalists "want to have power over their workplace and their careers," says WGAE's Peterson. "It's one thing to say, 'I want the rules to be rational.' They also want to help make the rules in the first place."

In other words, workers are motivated to democratize their newsrooms. As one organizer puts it, "I think they felt good about the work they were doing, but they wanted more of a voice and control over the direction the company was going in." Journalists turning to unions as a way to formalize workers' voices has been driven by a "deeply held belief that the more democratic that our workplace is, the more receptive it will be to input that could produce better journalism," says a journalist-organizer.

Redistributing power

The voice option is accessed through collective action. Digital journalists have come to recognize that the problems they confront are in no small part a product of negotiating with their employer individually. As Nolan writes in the Gawker post we quote at the start of this chapter, "A union is . . . the only real mechanism that enables employees to join together to bargain collectively, rather than as a bunch of separate, powerless entities."[15] And over the next few years, hundreds of journalists in dozens of newsrooms would demonstrate their agreement, proving that "movement" is more apt than "wave" to describe the union push in digital media. Framing digital media unions as a movement also acknowledges the networks of solidarity that, as we argue in later chapters, support journalists union organizing campaigns. Journalists hold no illusions that unionizing is a panacea, but they recognize nonetheless that a union can be, in one media worker's words, "a living and breathing mechanism to distribute power more evenly."

Notes

1 Hamilton Nolan, "Why We've Decided to Organize," *Gawker*, April 16, 2015, https://gawker.com/why-weve-decided-to-organize-1698246231.
2 See: John Kelly, *Rethinking Industrial Relations: Mobilization, Collectivism and Long Waves* (London and New York: Routledge, 1998); Marie-Josée Legault and Johanna Weststar, "The Capacity for Mobilization in Project-Based Cultural Work: A Case of the Video Game Industry," *Canadian Journal of Communication* 49 (2015): 203–21.
3 John Kelly and Vidu Badigannavar, "Union Organizing," in *Union Organizing and Activity*, eds. John E. Kelly and Paul Willman (London: Routledge, 2004), 33.
4 Kelly, *Rethinking Industrial Relations*, 27.
5 Kelly and Badigannavar, "Union Organizing," 33.
6 Kelly, *Rethinking Industrial Relations*, 25.
7 Kelly, *Rethinking Industrial Relations*, 29.
8 Javiera Quintana in Labor Video Project, "Democracy Depends on Journalism, Journalism Depends on the Union: Digital Media Workers Speak Out," panel at Labor Notes conference, Chicago, April 17, 2018, www.youtube.com/watch?v=wAaoIjjPRto.
9 Richard Wells, "Connecting the Dots: Labor and the Digital Landscape," *Labor: Studies in Working Class History* 15, no. 3 (2018): 67.
10 Melissa Gregg, *Work's Intimacy* (Cambridge: Polity Press, 2011), 2–3.
11 Jane McAlevey, *No Shortcuts: Organizing for Power in the New Gilded Age* (Oxford: Oxford University Press, 2016), 1.

12 Albert O. Hirschman, *Exit, Voice, and Loyalty: Responses to Decline in Firms, Organizations, and States* (Cambridge: Harvard University Press, 1970), 33.

13 Hirschman, *Exit, Voice, and Loyalty*, 30.

14 See Doris Ruth Eikhof and Chris Warhurst, "The Promised Land? Why Social Inequalities are Systemic in the Creative Industries," *Employee Relations* 35, no. 5 (2013): 495–508.

15 Nolan, "Why We've Decided to Organize."

2   Activation

Galvanizing moments

Around Christmas 2016, Vox Media's People & Culture department (Vox-speak for Human Resources) alerted employees via Slack that pay days would move from the first and fifteenth of the month to the seventh and twenty-second. "There was sort of a meltdown in Slack," says a Vox journalist. The company remedied the change for staff who needed it, but the incident was symptomatic of several employees' broader concerns. The person watching the Slack "meltdown" had thought for some time that Vox needed a union. The sudden payday move cemented concern that Vox had "changed from a scrappy start-up where everyone does everything and there aren't really rules or boundaries . . . to 'now we're a real corporation.'"

Similar sentiments emerged at Thrillist earlier that year, when CEO Ben Lerer announced a $100 million investment from Discovery and the merger of Thrillist and four other sites into Group Nine Media. The announcement made staff uneasy; they expected structural change and layoffs to follow. "I immediately saw the writing on the wall," says a Thrillist journalist. The investment "was framed as this great thing, but it never came with . . . people getting raises . . . there [was] no tangible benefit other than [Lerer] made a lot of money." Staff wanted a way "to at least assert a little bit of control and have a little bit of say in our employment and in how our employer treats us." Workers across the company's two offices, including remote workers, had been discussing unionization, but it wasn't until Lerer's next big announcement, the layoffs of 20 people, that the drive bounded forward. Layoffs were "a galvanizing moment," says a Thrillist organizer, and propelled the organizing committee toward publicly announcing their union bid.

Singular events ranging in scale kick-started simmering union drives: changes to weekend working practices at ThinkProgress; the enforcement of non-compete contracts at Law360; a union-negotiated raise for British journalists at *The Guardian* not available to their US counterparts; the firing of a journalist "unexpectedly . . . and with no recourse" at RawStory; and sudden layoffs at a range of companies. While BuzzFeed Canada journalists had toyed with the idea of unionizing, it took BuzzFeed cutting 15 percent of its staff—over 200 people—in January 2019 to spark an official bid, which workers launched alongside drives by the US and German offices. Sensing safety in numbers, a journalist group-texted her colleagues (only six are eligible to be in the union) to see who wanted to unionize. "Unionization was a response to this . . . feeling of, 'oh, crap, this industry is collapsing and we could be next, and we need to get a handle on this,'" she says.

While journalists had been discussing problems such as pay disparities, management transparency, and needing a voice in decision-making (see Chapter 1), for many it took a trigger to move from shared collective grievances to activating a union drive. This chapter examines the second phase of the larger organizing process: activation, when workers move from diagnosing collective problems to launching a full-fledged union bid. We document a collection of galvanizing movements that crystallized workers' grievances—solidifying the distinction between "us" and "them"—and the broader contextual and structural conditions that enabled journalists to unionize. A multiplicity of factors interacted to activate the recent wave of unionization, including digital media workers' developing class consciousness; the volatility of the industry; employment relationships that enabled legal access to unions; the presence of unions ready and willing to organize that fit journalists' conceptions of themselves as workers; and a political climate in the United States that, for this constituency, contributes to a renewal of social critique and collective sensibility.

Class consciousness

Over the past decade or so, digital media has grown from a "boot-strappy" collection of blogs, independent sites, and small companies into an established, profitable, and expanding sector, comprised of digital-first and legacy media companies alike.[1] Digital outlets have consolidated as giants like Univision, Disney, Viacom, and Comcast acquire or invest in smaller sites. Several of the digital newsrooms that unionized are independently owned, but many are part of established media conglomerates or have grown into large, powerful companies. The Huffington Post, which co-founder Arianna Huffington sold to AOL in 2011, became part of telecom conglomerate Verizon in 2015 when it bought AOL (it's now called HuffPost). MTV News is owned by multinational Viacom. Vox Media has seven separate "verticals"—an industry term for stand-alone sites aimed at distinct audiences—plus a collection of platforms and other business services, and in 2019 acquired New York Media, which publishes *New York* magazine and several websites. Group Nine Media emerged from combining five small media sites, including Thrillist and The Dodo (now both unionized), and investors include Discovery Communications and Axel Springer, the largest digital publisher in Europe. Thrillist's CEO, Ben Lerer, is the son of venture capitalist Kenneth Lerer, who co-founded the Huffington Post and had a stint as BuzzFeed's chairman. Despite tumult in the industry, digital media is "big business, and people are making a tremendous amount of money from the work that's done in this industry," says a journalist-organizer. "It would be nice if there was a more equitable distribution of that wealth."

Such a read of digital media challenges the narrative of economic crisis that has plagued journalism for well over a decade now and frames journalists' desire for redistributive justice in sectoral terms. At the start of the union wave, digital media workers watched as investments poured into their outlets, execs posted high profits, and companies expanded. Workers grew increasingly impatient with management claims of minimal resources. When her employer balked at the request of a $2,000 starting salary increase, one journalist-organizer thought, "the money is there; you're just not giving it to me." Journalists questioned the uncertainty and insecurity they felt as news headlines clarified the power divide between workers and their wealthy bosses: soon after 20 Thrillist workers were laid off, Ben Lerer's $7.4 million New York apartment went on the market,[2] angering employees "struggling in an outer-borough neighbourhood to make it," says a journalist. During the Vice campaign, media frequently profiled then-CEO Shane Smith's lavish lifestyle. "It is very galling to be working and making effectively $15 an hour, so below a livable wage in Toronto, and then to see news of the CEO of your company buying a $23 million mansion," says a Vice Canada organizer.[3] *Los Angeles Times* journalists read about then-owner Tronc's board paying millions per year for a private jet while employees were food insecure and struggling to pay for housing. "It was astonishing to hear," says one organizer, who continues:[4]

> When you see the chairman of your company's board is paying millions of dollars to rent a jet from his own company, that really moved people in the newsroom to see that things don't have to be this way. This is not a problem of the industry, this is a problem with industry executives.

Naming the class disparities between media workers and those who profit from their labor has been a vital element in activating the wave of union drives. Unions were not a foregone conclusion in this industry. Though generally pro-union, many journalists struggled to reconcile their impressions of unions with their own professional self-conception. Before she became a key organizer and active union member, for example, a Vice Canada worker thought that "unions are for people who work in factories, where, you know, a machine could fall on you; you need union protection" (as we show in Chapter 4, management reinforced this message). To unionize, digital media workers had to collectively challenge a range of assumptions about their work and occupational identity, including the individual competitiveness and entrepreneurialism on which neoliberal capitalism thrives; the professional, detached observer status historically linked to journalists; and the influence on digital media generally of Silicon Valley's "Californian ideology," a heady mix of techno-libertarianism and free market credo that has, until recently, helped stave off unionization in high tech sectors.[5] Until he saw other digital outlets go union, one journalist-organizer says he hadn't "really considered that there was [an] option in the form of collective bargaining." Normally, his response to workplace frustrations would have been to "quit or suck it up." But when a company flaunts its economic success, workers' bargaining power potentially builds.

The impulse to "quit or suck it up" is a more typical response to workplace challenges than launching a union drive. Research on young workers' propensity to organize shows that generally young workers—roughly 18–35-year-olds—have a "slight positive orientation" to unions, but lack experience with and knowledge about unions, so don't normally consider joining, let alone organizing one.[6] The Pew Research Center found that a majority of Americans aged 18–29 surveyed in 2018–68 percent—hold positive views of unions.[7] Still, it's more typical for young workers to exit jobs rather than voice their concerns or act collectively,[8] reflecting a lack of attachment to their workplaces and a lack of experience with labor unions, often because unions have not tried to organize the sectors in which young people work. But digital media workers maintain deep commitments to their jobs, to working in journalism long-term, and often to the companies for which they work.

The digital media workers who organized unions also have an advantage over many of the young-worker subjects in sociological research on propensity to organize: employment relationships. The digital media workers who unionized are employed on a continuous basis for one employer, and are therefore legally entitled to access a framework of collective bargaining rights in North America. Unions have fought to include workers employed through third-party staffing agencies in bargaining units, such as at *The New Yorker*, where subcontracted fact checkers were converted to full-time staff thanks to The New Yorker Union's organizing on the issue.[9] Precarious forms of employment—subcontracted, part-time, temporary, freelance, casual, on-demand, misclassified, and seasonal—are a major challenge for collectively organizing vast swaths of the labor force. Although the use of freelancers and contractors is widespread in digital media, the core workforce remains employees with legal rights to unionize and collectively bargain. So, when journalists were ready to take the leap, the Writers Guild of America, East (WGAE) and the NewsGuild jumped at the chance to organize.

Doubling down

The WGAE had been eyeing the digital media sector for years before Gawker became its first digital-only unit. The WGAE has historically been a screenwriters' union. It grew out of the Screen Writers Guild, formed in 1933 by "playwrights, journalists, and novelists who were lured to Hollywood to write dialogue for talkies."[10] In 1954, the Guild transformed into the Writers Guild of America, West and the Writers Guild of America, East. The WGAE began strategizing around digital technologies during the 2007–2008 Writers Guild of America strike, when 12,000 screenwriters struck for 100 days over payments for digital distribution and the reuse of scripted content in digital form. Screenwriters wanted contract coverage for born-digital texts—unchartered territory in Hollywood at the time—and the union had to rethink protections for writers, as digital technologies were about to transform production and business models.[11]

After the strike, the WGAE launched an initiative called Writers Guild 2.0 to determine what organizing and representing writers who create digital content would mean. The union realized "there's this thing called the internet, and there's writing that happens there," says an organizer hired after the strike to grow the WGAE's digital base. Organizers began holding panels, skills trainings, and meetings with creators and industry players to understand the shifting digital landscape. Through a caucus model, the union could connect with non-member writers by holding professional development, discussion, and networking events aimed at addressing industry-wide issues rather than targeting a particular employer—an approach the WGAE organizer calls "community building." During this period, the union organized a few small outlets that create online content and difficult-to-organize freelancers producing reality TV.[12] While the WGAE has for some time represented news journalists at public TV stations, local affiliates, CBS, and ABC, it didn't have sights on the emergent digital journalism sector until Vice Media began producing scripted video content.

By 2014, Vice had transformed from a counter-culture magazine into a global media giant with a slate of websites, an HBO show, a record label, and an in-house ad agency.[13] It had secured millions of dollars in investments from Rupert Murdoch, A&E (owned by Disney and Hearst), and venture-capital funds, pushing its valuation to $2.5 billion.[14] As then-CEO Shane Smith publicly flaunted his wealth, media reported on difficult working conditions in Vice offices, low salaries (in the $20,000-$30,000 range in New York), and editorial capitulation to corporate sponsors.[15] So, when it began producing more video content at the end of 2014, Vice became a prime target for WGAE. Vice's image consciousness and publicly progressive stance made the company a strategic choice: "opposing a union would be a bad look" for Vice, says a WGAE organizer. Vice's brand became "a leverage strategy to get them to recognize a union."

Initial conversations with video creators led nowhere ("there was a lot of fear," says an organizer), so the union switched tactics and began researching the company's financial operations. A WGAE organizer named Ursula Lawrence asked Gawker's Hamilton Nolan if he would report on Vice's suspected misuse of state subsidies for the site, as Nolan was effectively on the Vice beat, exposing working conditions in a string of articles.[16] During their conversations, Nolan said to Lawrence, "why don't you try to organize us?" Nolan was attuned to labor issues in the sector and often encountered reader comments asking why Gawker staff weren't unionized. "For a long time, I thought it was sort of beside the point for workplaces like this to unionize," Nolan told us. "I thought it wasn't as important as [unionizing] low wage workers. . . . As time went on, I came to realize that [unions] should be a basic feature of the workplace."

Lawrence was intrigued, but didn't think unionizing Gawker was possible. "At that point, we hadn't organized anything that was just text on a screen," she says. There was also a concern about jurisdiction, whether a union that traditionally represented film and television writers would be encroaching on the NewsGuild's territory. But unionizing Gawker Media was too good an opportunity to pass up, so Nolan set a meeting at the WGAE's office, invited all Gawker Media staff via Facebook, and 40 people showed up. The union was surprised by the turnout and by journalists' enthusiasm. "That this was a group of people who in five days could get [40] people in a room . . . that was really exciting," says Lawrence. Organizers didn't realize the broader potential to organize this sector until the day Gawker Media's union was recognized. "That's when it really began to dawn on us," says Lawrence. "We received several calls and emails almost immediately from people at other publications, and we were like, 'wow.'"

NewsGuild organizers don't like hearing that Gawker was the first digital news outlet to unionize. Locals of the NewsGuild won the first contract for a "stand-alone on-line news organization" in 1999 for journalists at Times Company Digital (the web arm of *The New York Times*), and represent workers at Truthout, The Daily Beast, and digital workers at *The Washington Post*.[17] In 2011, the Guild supported the National Writers Union in a strike by non-unionized freelance writers against the Huffington Post, whose lack of payment for writers seemed outrageous after AOL's $315 million purchase.[18] But the NewsGuild's primary constituents have been newspaper journalists, so over the past few decades, the union has focused on defending existing contracts as the newspaper industry has been gutted: between 2008 and 2017, 23 percent of newsroom jobs in all media in the United States were lost, and newspaper jobs dropped by 45 percent.[19] Although NewsGuild organizers had been in contact with journalists in a couple of digital newsrooms over the years, overall, "there wasn't a large-scale commitment to organizing," says an organizer. That changed in July 2015, when Guardian US journalists unionized with the NewsGuild of New York. In October, digital journalists at the now-closed Al Jazeera America also voted to unionize with the NewsGuild of New York. These drives, paired with the buzz around Gawker's campaign and the WGAE's official entry into journalism, fueled resolve in the NewsGuild to build and fund a digital strategy, and it received a $500,000 internal grant from parent union the Communication Workers of America to organize digital journalists.[20]

An unspoken but "undeniable competition" exists between the two unions, notes journalist Steven Greenhouse, an upshot of which has been "intensified and accelerated efforts to unionize journalists."[21] To date, well over 2,000 new media union members have joined the labor movement, an exhilarating feat for organizers not accustomed to winning. Says a News-Guild organizer:

> We were in this kind of defensive posture for so long, fighting all of the cuts to newspapers. So much of the focus was taken away from organizing and more on protecting what we have, what we have left. So, for the union to really double down and put more resources into organizing now and to have so many hot shops, where workers are coming to us, kicking down the door to organize. It's not something you experience very often as an organizer, as a union. It's a really exciting time.

Both unions see organizing digital media as an extension of the work they have always done: protecting and representing writers and journalists as industries adopt or adapt to new technologies, and defending journalism from corporate attacks. The NewsGuild has existed since 1933, weathering enormous transformations in the industry over the decades. Early US efforts to unionize journalists in the late 19th and early 20th centuries failed for a range of reasons, but a major obstacle was what historians call an "ideology of newswork," which positioned journalism as intellectual, individualistic work irreconcilable with the collectivism of organized labor and militant actions such as strikes.[22] It wasn't until 1933, when the US Congress passed the *National Industrial Recovery Act* (NIRA) to stimulate economic recovery, that journalists formed a lasting union.[23] Among other provisions designed to decrease unemployment, the NIRA included hour and wage provisions for editorial workers. In response, publishers lobbied for reporters to be classified as professionals, as the NIRA exempted professionals from regulated working hours.[24] This outraged journalists, whose material conditions—wages, hours, and general treatment—didn't reflect professional status. After much organizing, and after famed *New York World Telegram* columnist Heywood Broun forcefully took up the cause of a national union, the American Newspaper Guild (ANG) was born.[25] The union expanded to Canada in the late 1940s, establishing the ANG as an international union,[26] and changed its name twice: to The Newspaper Guild in the early 1970s, responding to pressure from growing Canadian membership, and then to The NewsGuild in 2015, to appeal to a broader range of media workers.

Over the decades, under parent union Communication Workers of America, branches of the union have experimented with innovative approaches to organizing. The Washington-Baltimore branch helped organize software engineers at Lanetix, drawing attention to the prospects of organizing tech workers. The Guild's Canadian counterpart, the Canadian Media Guild (CMG), runs an Associate Members program, essentially free proto-union membership to emerging media workers, students, and the precariously employed. The program provides training, mentorship, and contract advice to members; advocates for media workers' rights; and has developed contract language on internships that was included in Vice Canada's first collective agreement. The CMG engages in similar "community building" tactics as the WGAE, hosting social events and panel discussions for non-union media workers as a way to "build relationships . . . so that we can start having a conversation with them about working conditions," says an organizer. The CMG also runs a freelance branch which, despite an uncertain future and staff shortage, represents freelance media workers who cannot join a union.[27] As for the WGAE, as Miranda Banks notes, the union has a history of strategically reshuffling priorities during times of economic and technological flux: "Often the Guild defines or refines its mission at key moments of crisis brought on by technological change and the revision of economic structures within the entertainment industry."[28]

Being propelled into organizing by keen and self-motivated journalists has energized and expanded both unions, particularly in New York City, generating a concentrated spark of renewal in a broader labor movement facing decades of attacks from capital and the state.[29] Although scholars and labor activists alike have mounted important criticisms of unions, particularly a tendency among many toward business or service unionism,[30] digital media workers' movement to organize demonstrates the ongoing necessity of unions. While the journalist-organizers we interviewed are generally pro-union, they knew little about how to run a union drive. They were motivated to organize but needed guidance on tactics and strategies, laws, and procedures. As we show in Chapter 3, digital media workers also needed a sense of autonomy and ownership in the organizing process, at times challenging union organizers' longstanding practices. They found in the WGAE and the NewsGuild the right combination of guidance and autonomy.

In the air

Digital union drives have been made possible by a confluence of triggers that spurred workers to act on their workplace grievances, by a developing class consciousness, and by access to unions willing to invest in organizing. Vital, too, has been the broader political and social climate that helped make a collective response in the form of labor unions seem attainable. There was "a certain amount of tension and knowledge in the air" that enabled people to examine their working conditions, says one journalist-organizer. The legacy of Occupy Wall Street and the 2016 Bernie Sanders presidential campaign legitimated discourses about economic inequality and calls for collective responses. Black Lives Matter and a re-energized feminist politics empowered journalists to link gender- and race-based grievances to structural problems in the industry and economy. Social movement organizing and discourse gave media workers' grievances weight, context, and perspective, and fueled a renewal of collective sensibility. "All of these movements are familiar to people in this space," explains a union staffer. Another organizer says that journalists who write regularly about social movements, politics, economic inequality, and unions are "already ideologically more available" to unions.

The journalists who did on-the-ground organizing in their newsrooms told us they generally found an openness toward unions among colleagues because, as one journalist says, "it's just very obvious to most of us that the way the economy works right now does not work for us." Another says, thanks to contemporary social movements, "it's a little more popular, or maybe more fashionable, to have a more overt political identity than it was previously." She continues: "within the reality we found ourselves . . . a union, to a lot of young people, is a good amalgamation of some very high-minded political principles and some very practical organizing." Another motivating factor was the 2016 election of Donald Trump as President of the United States. Journalists worried that media would become a political target, and believed that workplace organizing was one way to "make change at a very overwhelming time," says an organizer. The morning after the election, an MTV News journalist posted a message to coworkers in Slack: "we need a union," expressing concern about affordable healthcare and legal protections under the new political regime. As another journalist notes, "politicians who vilify the free press also make it a lot easier to stand together."

Many journalists we interviewed were motivated by the momentum of shop after shop announcing union drives and winning. Seeing their peers— mostly young workers in youth-oriented media outlets—successfully organize made unionization seem possible, if not inevitable. Watching union density build in digital media convinced a Vox organizer that unionizing "is the single most important thing that any digital media company could do right now, at least from a worker perspective." While many cite Gawker's very public drive as the moment that launched dozens of campaigns, others deny the Gawker drive had influence. Yet, says one organizer, "you can't really downplay the significance of [Gawker's] . . . splashy, sexy campaign for these young digital workers."

Considering specific workplace grievances in such a politically charged context shows why digital journalists have unionized. The case of digital journalists' unions demonstrates that workers do push back when they are squeezed, even workers in highly individualistic, competitive industries, where people are hired for their social media followings and when a labor surplus means there's always someone willing to work for less. "When the pendulum swings toward the commodification of labor, it provokes strong countermovements demanding protection," writes labor scholar Beverly Silver.[31] As we outlined in Chapter 1, for digital media workers, the pendulum swung toward the commodification of their individual labor power and of journalism itself. Marxist analysis, argues Silver, shows that as the organization of production changes, "new agencies and sites of conflict emerge along with new demands and forms of struggle, reflecting the shifting terrain on which labor-capital relations develop."[32] Because journalism is still overwhelmingly produced as a commodity under contemporary capitalism, class struggle persists, and "new sites of investment"[33] become sites of conflict. As Richard Wells argues, journalism is not an exception to "the general rule of struggle between labor and capital"; it's just that researchers, commentators, and journalists rarely describe media work in such terms.[34]

The process of collective organizing pushed digital media workers to shift their thinking beyond individual conditions to address structural power in the workplace, to enact the theory that improvements require collective action. One journalist-organizer explains this shift in thinking:

> [I]f someone was getting paid really low, they often would think it was just them, and that they hadn't negotiated hard enough, and they hadn't

tried hard enough. . . . But then you realize other people were getting paid just as low. . . . [F]or the vast majority of us, it took joining forces to feel like we had any sort of power.

And that is the aim of collective organizing: to transform outrage over a specific injustice or complaint—low pay, a change in pay period, unexpected layoffs—into a vehicle to address structural inequality and boost workers' power.[35] As Silver writes, "mobilizations over the past century have been fueled by the belief that workers do indeed have power and, moreover, that their power can be used to effectively transform their conditions of work and life for the better."[36] Several journalists we interviewed say launching a union drive was a way to do *something* to address the unequal power relations they see all around them. "This is just . . . a drop in the ocean . . . [but] it's the only thing I really know how to do," says a journalist-organizer. Unionizing was one way he felt he could address not just problems in his workplace, but "the wave of inequality that everyone talks about. This growing gap between people who can just scare up a hundred million dollars and . . . the people who are living paycheck to paycheck." He acknowledges that he is not in "the same kind of worker-class that unions are traditionally associated with," but is organizing in solidarity with all workers. And, he says, "hopefully it'll work."

Notes

1 Hamilton Nolan, cited in Jason Farbman, "Organizing New Media," *Jacobin*, November 17, 2016, www.jacobinmag.com/2016/11/gawker-union-gizmodo-deadspin-organized-labor-online-univision-writers-guild/.
2 Michelle Cohen, "Thrillist Co-Founder Ben Lerer Lists Colorful, Pop Art-Filled Soho Loft for $7.4M," *6SQFT*, February 13, 2017, www.6sqft.com/thrillist-co-founder-ben-lerer-lists-colorful-pop-art-filled-soho-loft-for-7-4m/.
3 See Madeline Stone, "VICE CEO Shane Smith Bought a Mansion in Santa Monica for $23 Million," *Business Insider*, August 10, 2015, www.businessinsider.com/vice-ceo-shane-smith-buys-santa-monica-mansion-for-23-million-2015-8.
4 Labor Video Project, "Democracy Depends on Journalism, Journalism Depends on the Union: Digital Media Workers Speak Out," panel at Labor Notes conference, Chicago, April 17, 2018, www.youtube.com/watch?v=wAaoIjjPRto.
5 Imre Szeman, "Entrepreneurship as the New Common Sense," *The South Atlantic Quarterly* 114, no. 3 (July 2015): 471–90; Mark Deuze, "What Is Journalism? Professional Identity and Ideology of Journalists Reconsidered," *Journalism* 6, no. 4 (2005): 443–65; Richard Barbrook and Andy Cameron, "The Californian Ideology," *Mute* 1, no. 3 (1995), www.metamute.org/editorial/articles/californian-ideology.
6 Richard Freeman and Wayne Diamond, "Young Workers and Trade Unions," in *Representing Workers: Trade Union Recognition and Membership in Britain*, eds. Howard Gospel and Stephen Wood (London: Routledge, 2003), 30; Andy

Hodder and Lefteris Krestos, "Young Workers and Unions: Context and Overview," in *Young Workers and Trade Unions: A Global View*, eds. Andy Hodder and Lefteris Krestos (New York: Palgrave Macmillan, 2015), 1–15.

7 Hannah Fingerhut, "More Americans View Long-Term Decline in Union Membership Negatively Than Positively," *Pew Research Center*, June 5, 2018, www.pewresearch.org/fact-tank/2018/06/05/more-americans-view-long-term-decline-in-union-membership-negatively-than-positively/.

8 Peter Haynes, Jack Vowles, and Peter Boxall, "Explaining the Younger-Older Worker Union Density Gap," *British Journal of Industrial Relations* 43, no. 1 (2005): 93–116.

9 Josh Eidelson, "New Yorker Fact-Checkers Win Employee Status after Union Push," *Bloomberg*, September 3, 2019, www.bloomberg.com/news/articles/2019-09-03/new-yorker-fact-checkers-win-employee-status-after-union-push.

10 Miranda J. Banks, "The Picket Line Online: Creative Labor, Digital Activism, and the 2007–2008 Writers Guild of America Strike," *Popular Communication* 8, no. 1 (2010): 21.

11 Banks, "The Picket Line Online."

12 Sarah Jaffe, "A Group of Workers Corporate America Claimed Were Impossible to Organize Win Key Union Votes," *AlterNet*, January 10, 2011, www.alternet.org/economy/149476/a_group_of_workers_corporate_america_claimed_were_impossible_to_organize_win_key_union_votes/.

13 Nicole S. Cohen and Greig de Peuter, "'I Work at VICE Canada and I Need a Union': Organizing Digital Media," in *Labour under Attack: Anti-Unionism in Canada*, eds. Stephanie Ross and Larry Savage (Halifax and Winnipeg: Fernwood, 2018), 114–28.

14 Reeves Wiedeman, "A Company Built on a Bluff," *New York*, June 10, 2018, http://nymag.com/daily/intelligencer/2018/06/inside-vice-media-shane-smith.html.

15 Hamilton Nolan, "Working at Vice Media Is Not as Cool as It Seems," *Gawker*, May 30, 2014, http://gawker.com/working-at-vice-media-is-not-as-cool-as-it-seems-1579711577.

16 Hamilton Nolan, "Working at Vice Media Is Not as Cool as It Seems"; Hamilton Nolan, "Here Is Vice Media's Salary Breakdown," *Gawker*, December 18, 2014, http://gawker.com/here-is-vice-medias-salary-breakdown-1672760767: Hamilton Nolan, "The Single Most Insufferable Response to Our Vice Media Story," *Gawker*, June 2, 2014, http://gawker.com/the-single-most-insufferable-response-to-our-vice-media-1584736050.

17 Newspaper Guild of New York, "Guild Negotiates First Contract at Times Company Digital," December 13, 1999, https://web.archive.org/web/20001206134000/http:/www.nyguild.org/loc006.htm; Errol Salamon, "Digital Media Workers Are Unionizing Like It's 1999," *CMG Freelance*, March 23, 2016, http://cmgfreelance.ca/en/digital-media-workers-are-unionizing-like-its-1999/.

18 Bill Lasarow, "AOL-Huffington Post: The Virtual Picket Line," *The Guardian*, March 28, 2011, www.theguardian.com/commentisfree/cifamerica/2011/mar/28/huffington-post-aol.

19 Elizabeth Grieco, "Newsroom Employment Dropped Nearly a Quarter in Less Than 10 Years, with Greatest Decline at Newspapers," *Pew Research Center*, July 30, 2018, www.pewresearch.org/fact-tank/2018/07/30/newsroom-employment-dropped-nearly-a-quarter-in-less-than-10-years-with-greatest-decline-at-newspapers/.

20 Peter Sterne, "News Guild Starts $500,000 Campaign to Organize Digital News-rooms," *Politico*, September 1, 2015, www.politico.com/media/story/2015/09/news-guild-starts-500-000-campaign-to-organize-digital-newsrooms-004198.

21 Steven Greenhouse, "More Secure Jobs, Bigger Paychecks," *Columbia Journalism Review* (Spring/Summer, 2018), www.cjr.org/special_report/media-unions-history.php/.

22 William S. Solomon, "The Site of Newsroom Labor: The Division of Editorial Practices," in *Newsworkers: Toward a History of the Rank and File*, eds. Hanno Hardt and Bonnie Brennen (Minneapolis: University of Minnesota Press, 1995), 128.

23 Daniel J. Leab, *A Union of Individuals: The Formation of the American Newspaper Guild, 1933–1936* (New York: Columbia University Press, 1970).

24 Broun Heywood, *It Seems to Me, 1925–1935* (New York: Harcourt, Brace and Company, 1935), 210; Leab, *A Union of Individuals*, 33, 75.

25 Leab, *A Union of Individuals*, 44.

26 Cecilia Deck, "History of the Newspaper Guild in Canada 1936–1986," in *Essays in Journalism*, ed. Heather Hiscox (London: University of Western Ontario, 1988), 15–34.

27 See Nicole S. Cohen, *Writers' Rights: Freelance Journalism in a Digital Age* (Montreal and Kingston: McGill-Queen's University Press, 2016).

28 Banks, "The Picket Line Online," 21.

29 Jane McAlevey, *No Shortcuts: Organizing for Power in the New Gilded Age* (Oxford: Oxford University Press, 2016), 17.

30 Stephanie Ross, "Varieties of Social Unionism: Towards a Framework for Comparison," *Just Labour: A Canadian Journal of Work and Society* 11 (2007): 16–34.

31 Beverly J. Silver, *Forces of Labor: Workers' Movements and Globalization since 1870* (Cambridge: Cambridge University Press, 2003), 17.

32 Silver, *Forces of Labor*, 19.

33 Silver, *Forces of Labor*, 5.

34 Richard Wells, "Connecting the Dots: Labor and the Digital Landscape," *Labor: Studies in Working Class History* 15, no. 3 (2018): 16.

35 McAlevey, *No Shortcuts*.

36 Silver, *Forces of Labor*, 16.

3 Mobilization

Not keeping your head down

In a volatile industry where staff positions are precious and personal brands can be a safety net, it's understandable that a young journalist, speaking shortly before the digital media union movement got rolling, admitted that the "barriers . . . to starting a union drive—and the inevitable stress and problems it would create—seem more onerous than keeping one's head down."[1] By 2019, journalists experienced a massive mood swing: workers at over 50 publications had unionized within four years. The mood is captured in a 16-second video @meeshkakim posted to Twitter on March 29, 2019. In it, two young women dance like no one is watching to Des'ree's empowerment anthem "You Gotta Be" in a public square in daytime Manhattan. The dancers hold a "Pitchfork Union" sign, announcing their campaign to unionize with the NewsGuild of New York.

This short video reveals a lot about organizing in digital media and beyond. First is the growing position in American union circles that "[i]f there is going to be a revival of the U.S. labor movement, it's likely that women are going to lead it."[2] Second is the embrace of social media platforms by journalists to publicize their unionization campaigns, to receive symbolic support from their professional peers, and, as an *L.A. Times* journalist-organizer puts it, to "[build] a direct relationship with our readers."[3] And third is the joy that can be found in collective action. As @meeshkakim wrote when she posted Pitchfork Union's letter requesting management recognition to Twitter, "my heart is swelling knowing that we have each others' backs on this."

This chapter examines how journalists organize unions, a multifaceted process we describe using the term mobilization. Labor researchers challenge the tendency to use "organizing" and "mobilizing" interchangeably, as doing so conflates distinct activities.[4] Jane McAlevey, for example, urges the union movement to restore a commitment to "deep organizing," in which "[o]rdinary people help make the power analysis, design the strategy, and achieve the outcome."[5] She reserves the term mobilizing for efforts to spur an already-committed group to take specific action, like a strike or a rally. Recognizing such differences, we use mobilization in this chapter to describe the many steps involved in a unionization campaign, most of which fit McAlevey's criteria for deep organizing. In digital media unionization, mobilization is a worker-led process of building support for collective representation, signing union cards (or formally tracking commitments to unionize), and requesting voluntary recognition from management or filing for a National Labor Relations Board (NLRB) election.

This chapter follows journalist-organizers' mobilizing efforts from early-stage musings to logistical planning, choosing a parent union, interacting with staff union organizers, engaging prospective bargaining-unit members, building support, and going public to request recognition. These activities don't necessarily proceed sequentially or smoothly, and no two successful campaigns have unfolded in the same way. Some were secretive, others highly public; some developed swiftly, others slowly; some followed long-standing organizing principles, others departed. And while "getting to yes" is the procedural objective of mobilization, the higher goal is to foster collective political capacity and to clarify what it is that workers are organizing for.[6]

We pay particular attention to two aspects of journalists' union drives: affect and communication. Journalist-organizers describe their experiences using words like confidence and empowerment, or stress and exhaustion, while a staff organizer describes the desire to organize as a considered impulse to "turn fear and anger into action and hope." Yet emotion, feelings, and affect are only rarely—explicitly at least—centered in studies of worker organizing,[7] even though affect, or "the power 'to affect and be affected,'"[8] is immediately evident in the organizing context. Fear, for example, may frustrate or fuel willingness to take collective action.[9] Affect surfaces in the expansion and contraction of workers' sense of what is possible in a given situation.

While emotion is experienced individually, affect operates relationally. It inhabits the zone of "*in-between-ness*" and names "forces or intensities . . . that pass body to body."[10] As Phoebe Moore writes, "when workers become conscious of affect, or their power to act, they also become conscious of their ability to impact one another and potentially to collectively challenge abuses at work."[11] At the crux of "affective organizing"[12] are social bonds, the generative yet fragile substance of "cultures of solidarity."[13] Rosemary Hennessy highlights the central role "affective relations" play in labor organizing: "Bonds of loyalty, camaraderie, and friendship, of competition, jealousy, and betrayal are seething presences that act on and meddle with the processes whereby the collective bonds are formed that enable people to take action."[14]

Affect is a vital force in digital media union drives, as is communication, or the social and material process of the production of meaning.[15] The experiences of digital media unions underscore the communicative constitution of organizing,[16] including face-to-face conversations, digitally networked planning, "collective action frames,"[17] publicly posted letters to management, social media expressions of solidarity between journalists and their publics—communication is the stuff of mobilizing. This communicative dimension also illuminates one of the defining features of many new media union drives: self-organization.[18] Journalists led card signing and exercised control over the public face of their campaigns, a political corollary of contemporary journalists' norms of professional autonomy, digital habitat, and communicative expertise.

"Union?"

Megan McRobert, Digital Media Field Representative at the WGAE, says workers tend to contact the union about organizing when they arrive at the "rational determination that there is no safety in hiding and hoping." For all but the earliest union drives, the path to this determination is not easy to separate from the unionization "wave" in digital media, which demonstrates affect's mobilizing force. Several journalists were influenced by the Gawker Media campaign. "If Gawker hadn't unionized and been so public about it and so vocal about it," says a Thrillist journalist, "I don't think I would have seen [organizing] as a viable option." Other drives had a similar effect. American Vice workers' campaign inspired their Canadian counterparts, and when Foreign Policy unionized, Fusion journalists mused, "Why not Fusion?" BuzzFeed Canada journalists felt confident unionizing once they knew their American and German colleagues were doing the same.

A union organizer jokes that the size of the bargaining unit in a newly unionized digital shop can be outnumbered by media stories about the campaign. But as the digital media union movement's profile has grown, so has journalists' confidence in collective action. Journalists say their peers' organizing efforts inspired, encouraged, and emboldened them. News about victories at other outlets widened unorganized journalists' horizon of possibility: "it made it seem like it was feasible for us," says a Vice journalist. This is an object lesson in what affect theorists call "joyful passions," or affect that expands one's capacity to act.[19] When colleagues express worry about the potential risks of organizing, journalists reassure them by citing the record of other successful campaigns. "It's not just us," a journalist-organizer told colleagues worried about being fired for organizing. "So don't be scared . . . we are part of a national pattern." A CMG organizer says that wins at other shops have helped "normalize" unionization among digital media workers. Indeed, over time, journalists haven't necessarily needed a "catastrophic" work event to broach organizing with their colleagues: "we were just looking around at other newsrooms that were having success and we were like, 'this seems like an important moment for our industry,'" says a worker who helped organize her newsroom.

Sometimes, the decision to initiate a union drive can be traced to the smallest utterance. Journalists at The Intercept, which reports on global resistance, were talking over drinks about how to make their work an even more effective counterforce in the Trump era. A colleague who had come from a unionized newsroom piped in with, "It sounds like what you guys could use is a union." When the Vice US drive broke, a Vice Canada journalist canvassed a colleague, "What do you think about it?" And when Vox staff were venting in a private Slack room, a journalist typed, "Union?" A few coworkers replied with approving emojis, and the journalist later emailed them: "Hey, I'm serious. . . . Does anyone know how to start this?"

Friendship is often the entry point for organizing conversations. Conversations "started with just friends or people you're most comfortable around socializing," recalls a journalist who organized at Fusion. Likewise, at Al Jazeera America, the journalists who instigated organizing were "concentrated in particular friend groups." In some small, close-knit shops, virtually the entire news team participated in early organizing conversations. More common, however, is that two or three journalists start the discussion and gradually grow a core group of supporters. This early period tends to be "hush hush" and "clandestine." Instigators are cautious about who to approach, usually starting with people they are confident will be receptive. Keeping a campaign underground is considered good organizing strategy because, says an organizer, "more things get out of your control once it's public." Journalists are also nervous about word getting out because they understand that the deck is stacked against labor. With livelihoods at stake, one journalist-organizer says, "we only approached people who we thought could be trusted in the early stages, because we were worried about retaliatory firing."

At the beginning, conversations with close colleagues centered on basic questions such as, "How do we feel about the work environment?" While discussions often started with "cathartic complaining" and scrutinizing management behavior, in terms of affect, what is vital about these early talks is the emergent sense of shared experience and common hopes. "It felt like stuff that I felt on a very singular level, like frustrations I had about pay . . . I just didn't have them independently, everyone was feeling them," says a journalist. The conversation can tip to action—"what if we actually tried to do something about it?"—by imagining what a union contract might be able to achieve. By breaking silences and fostering bonds, these formative exchanges illustrate an enduring lesson: "it is only by turning to our fellow workers that we may realize—as has been the case for every class formation . . . —this [feeling of impasse is] not a condition we need to face alone."[20]

Although it didn't dissuade them from unionizing, most of the people who led organizing drives had little or no previous organizing experience. "We were very much novices going into this," says a journalist. Only a few people we spoke to fit into the "militant minority,"[21] the certainty of their political commitments reflected in statements like, "if you have a boss, you need a union." Still, several journalists began the organizing process with strong views on the importance of unions and sought out colleagues who shared their perspectives. "We felt like you needed the real true believers at the beginning or [things] could quickly fall apart," says a journalist-organizer. Journalists who spearheaded organizing drives are quick to articulate the importance of unions: "they are the only body explicitly designed to help workers," says the person who kicked off the Vice Canada drive. "If you don't have a union," says one of the organizers of Gawker's campaign, "you're never going to be able to negotiate as equals with your employer." And an MTV News organizer describes unionization as a "way of building the infrastructure that supports and protects people so they are capable of doing their best work."

Even without pre-formed political commitments to unions, journalists in core organizing groups emphasize the need for class politics in a no-collar workplace, where workers are more likely to express passion rather than lament for their work and loyalty rather than disdain for brands they work for. Journalist-organizers emphasized to colleagues that "you need . . . someone to have your back and . . . it's not going to be your boss, no matter how cool they are," says Kim Kelly, who organized at Vice. Her statement is a version of a recurring mobilizing narrative in digital media organizing: namely, that journalists' social bonds with each other, rather than individualized relationships with managers or owners, are their strongest resource to support their interests, needs, and aspirations.

Building relations

Once a core organizing group is formed, journalists contact potential parent unions. Although anti-union rhetoric frames a union as an infiltrating force, it's typically journalists themselves who initiate contact with a union, just one indicator of workers' self-organization. Routes to union contact vary. For example, after receiving a "get-over-it"-type response from a manager to voicing an editorial-process problem, one journalist completed a contact form on the WGAE website and received a call back from an organizer. "I left to hide in the alleyway behind the office to [take] the phone call," she says, "and just yelled it all out." In most cases, however, the decision to contact a union is made collectively.

Several factors shape which parent union journalists choose. Workers consider the outlets that the NewsGuild and the WGAE already represent and tend to favor the union they feel has "organized shops most like ours," as one journalist puts it. Because it organized Gawker Media, the WGAE has enjoyed first-mover advantages, particularly at digital-only publications. Other journalists, such as those at The Guardian US, were attracted to the NewsGuild's experience with large, established news organizations like *The New York Times* and international groups like the Associated Press. Journalist-organizers also rely on their professional networks, seeking out recommendations from trusted unionized colleagues.

Journalists decide on a union after instigators, the core group, or a wider cross-section of staff meet with a union organizer. Organizers' personal attributes are a decisive factor in choosing a union. "She just got it . . . she knew journalists . . . she knew production," says a Vice Canada journalist about the CMG organizer they met. In addition to familiarity with the field, organizers' supportiveness and enthusiasm are among the affective traits that journalists value in a staff organizer. Their communicative abilities are essential, too. As one journalist says about a preliminary meeting with a WGAE organizer, "She listened to us, and that was honestly probably the most important thing. We only got more confident in our feelings that this was the most appropriate avenue." The union's organizing principles also influence journalists' decisions. "What the newsroom really understood was that you needed to educate people on *why* a union, and [NewsGuild organizers] were willing to provide . . . help . . . on what the benefits of unionization were and slowly bring in people and teach them," says a journalist-organizer. "We actually need expertise. Otherwise, who needs the big parent union?"

So, while journalists are self-organized in that they initiate contact with a parent union to launch a drive, they rely on external support to advance their mobilization efforts. At union offices and nearby bars and restaurants, journalists' meetings with staff organizers clarify the latter's role, at the heart of which is "relation-building."[22] As a NewsGuild organizer explains, her involvement begins by "sitting down with a group at the onset and getting an idea of what the issues are, what really matters to people, asking a lot of questions, and really listening, spending a lot of time getting to know workers." In the process, organizers establish trust, gauge capacity, and assess opportunity so to not "[push] a campaign forward if there isn't a strong base," says one journalist.

The relationship between staff and inside organizers relies on mutual learning. Union staff explain to journalists "what you needed to do to get recognition," from outlining workers' legal rights to determining the bargaining unit, showing sample contracts, explaining how management might react, and "providing experience around [tactics] that have worked." A main goal of this training is to prepare inside organizers for the next step of their campaign: talking to colleagues, some of whom they have never spoken to before, about unionization. An organizer sums up his role: "it's really helping facilitate communication."

From there, the inside organizing committee internally executes the campaign, recruits colleagues, and liaises with staff organizers. Committee structure and composition varies. For example, Gothamist staff was small, so workers didn't feel a "need to have leaders who were doing massively more work than everyone else and leading this charge." In contrast, at Thrillist, 15 people served on the committee to organize an approximately 75-member bargaining unit. When building a committee, says a union organizer, best practice is aiming for "10 percent of the workforce, and a group that really represents all the dynamics of the newsroom . . . in job title, age, race, sex . . . to make sure we have a good and diverse group." While inside committees aim to include multiple departments and verticals, some journalists admit that their committees were ad hoc or self-selecting, "essentially people who were enthusiastic" and could devote time to the drive. Women and women of color led a number of campaigns, yet many committees remained predominately white. "It would be fantastic if we can have [the committees] represent ethnic and racial diversity," says a NewsGuild organizer, "but unfortunately, it just does not exist in these newsrooms, and that's part of what we're organizing around."

One journalist says organizing her newsroom helped "fight back" some of journalism's competitive and individualistic impulses. Being on the inside committee, says another, was "really empowering, because it felt like I could be productive with my frustrations at Vice and do something that would benefit the entire office." On the parent union side, organizers from all of the main unions—CMG, NewsGuild, WGAE—highlight inside committees' enthusiasm and engagement. "We did learn really quickly that people wanted ownership," says the WGAE's Lowell Peterson. As we will see, some tensions arose from this dynamic, but organizers maintain that devolving power to workers can lead to a "stronger organizing drive" and workers who "feel more part of the union," Peterson says. A high level of worker participation in the campaign can also have a lasting impact on the character of the unions journalists create. As a NewsGuild organizer puts it, "the culture established during the organizing is the culture that will reproduce itself through time."

Radiating outward

Reflecting a culture of self-organization, journalists lead card signing efforts. Whether a drive culminates in a secret ballot, card-check, or voluntary recognition, the term card signing designates the process of tracking support for collective representation. The NLRB accepts paper or electronic union cards, so unions use both paper and online cards during drives. First, organizers need to figure out who is eligible to be in the bargaining unit. This can be straightforward in small newsrooms, where people know their colleagues and it's obvious who represents management. It can be tricky, however, in companies that are larger, integrate multiple media production roles, employ remote workers, and have high workforce churn. To build their list of prospective unit members, for example, Vice Canada journalists had to scour LinkedIn after realizing their employer's staff directory was out of date. Organizers' lists identify the coworkers they need to mobilize, and how many people are needed to trigger an election (40 percent of unit members in Ontario, for example) or to show a majority.

Digital journalism drives, says a union organizer, follow "Organizing 101": "get to the personal conversations." One-on-one, worker-to-worker communication has been integral to the campaigns. "It is always much more impactful," explains a staff organizer, "when the person talking to you has the same understanding of the workplace, they have the same skin in the game." It's within peer-to-peer discussions that the social bonds underpinning collective labor organization form. Says another staff organizer, "Workers need to build the union through the organizing process. . . . If a staff organizer comes in and just gets the card signed, no worker power or capacity is being built."

Card signing unfolds through a hub-and-spoke network of communication, with inside committee members incrementally "radiating outward" among coworkers. Says a Fusion organizer, "we split up . . . people we knew in the company that we would feel comfortable putting out feelers to," and then individuals would report back to the committee. Beginning with colleagues they intuit would be most open to unionizing, committees leverage their "social circles" and their work roles. One editor's job, for instance, enabled her to serve as a bridge to offices in different cities, while a podcast producer's collaborative routine provided her not only with contacts across departments, but also cover for surreptitious meetings. Inside organizers "grow the circle gradually," strategically leaving people who they think will be least interested to the end, partly to reduce the risk of the campaign being leaked to management.

Given their digital habitat, journalists' mobilizing methods have been surprisingly analog during this phase. Communicating digitally makes it "easy for people to ignore you. . . . We had to meet with people," says a journalist-organizer. Organizers use nonwork email, Google chat, and direct messages via personal social media accounts to initiate contact with coworkers. Their messages are short and instrumental: "Hey, do you have a second to chat?" or, "This is happening, I don't know if you're aware. Let's meet for coffee." In keeping with the organizing ethos to meet people where they're comfortable, one-on-ones are held at cafés and bars, easing people's wariness of "the paper trail that you leave when you do things online," says a journalist.

At these meetings, journalist-organizers "gently" sound people out. One journalist emphasizes the importance of avoiding rhetorical formula. "One of the things that I learned early on in the drive," she says, was "not to launch into some sort of pitch, as if it were going to work with . . . different people every time." She modulated her script on the fly. If a colleague said they enjoyed their work, she might say, "Cool, so, we're talking about forming a union so we can lock in some of the stuff that's really, really good about working here right now," whereas if they complained about pay, she might adjust the rationale: "we were thinking about forming a union so that we can negotiate salary minimums." Most essential to these preliminary conversations, say staff organizers, is creating space for questions, not just offering a blunt, "are you in?" Ideally, inside organizers engage coworkers in meaningful dialogue, says a staff organizer: "What's going on for them? What does a union mean? What does the process look like?"

Organizers hold larger group meetings to provide updates, discuss strategy, and field questions as campaigns advance. Still, it can be a challenge to reach and inform all colleagues. At Gawker Media, for example, some workers ultimately voted against the union because they felt they "weren't communicated with enough," says an organizer. Other campaigns tried to avoid this scenario. Says an Intercept organizer, especially given the site's mission, "there's no excuse to not [organize] as democratically as possible. . . . We really were striving for vigorous, unanimous consent." Inclusiveness was particularly challenging in shops with remote workers. To keep geographically dispersed staff informed and engaged, a Fusion organizer put his professional skills to work: "I would . . . set up instant message threads and just basically live-blog the meeting for everyone. . . . It's something I do anyway as a reporter. So, I would just rapidly type out my notes. . . . I could take pictures of stuff and send it to the threads." Fusion's unionization, he says, would have been impossible without a "digital communication strategy."

Organizers and journalists have clashed, at times, around communication. One aspect of organizing communication is tracking support for the union to determine if organizers have sufficient numbers to win an election. Union staff were reluctant when journalists wanted, for example, to log yesses, nos, and maybes via a shared Google doc. Generally, admits McRobert, union staff "lock that shit down," so nothing leaks to management. But journalists are accustomed to and want access and transparency. Such expectations, coupled with new technologies, have shifted roles traditionally performed by staff organizers. "I'm not going to argue with a journalist over 'you have to meet with me in person, then I'm going to give you a paper list, then I have to take it back,' McRobert says. "They're going to be like, 'Cool, I work in Chicago, I'm done with this organizing effort, it's not going to work.'" Enabling journalists to track support is not simply a practical measure to help parent unions cope with dispersed workers and a heavy campaign workload. It's also a mode of trust and of recognizing that worker autonomy from the parent union within the organizing process is a vital pillar of successful campaigns.

On the whole, journalist-organizers say their coworkers were receptive to the idea of unionizing. Says a Vox organizer, "I talked to dozens and dozens of people, and a lot were really enthusiastic, some were iffy but we talked it out, and at worst, people were just apathetic." This range of responses was similar in all of the drives in our study. Supportive responses were encouraging, but, admits one journalist-organizer, "there were plenty of people on the fence." Misgivings are expressed in different guises in organizing conversations: anecdotes of a negative experience in a previous unionized workplace, concerns that going union might compromise journalistic objectivity, and assumptions that unions protect seniority to a fault, undermine flexibility, make workplaces bureaucratic, and could impose a pay cap. One journalist-organizer acknowledges that it was challenging yet essential to maintain composure in the face of detractors, knowing "at the end of the day, we were all going to still have to work together, whether the campaign succeeds or not."

For the most part, though, journalist-organizers confronted hesitation rather than outright anti-union hostilities. "Will management find out that I'm involved?" was the most popular question. A journalist-organizer describes some coworkers "who . . . ideologically supported the idea of a union, who even understood why we needed one, but were terrified of inciting some sort of bad response from management." The main worry was job loss, be it a vindictive target firing, mass layoffs, or owners regarding a union "as one headache too many and [deciding], 'fuck it, we're spinning them off,'" says a journalist. In a media labor economy organized around reputation, networks, and relationships, the label "troublemaker" is "scary for people unsure of future job prospects," says an organizer.

Acknowledging vulnerability while working to overcome fear is a core challenge of affective organizing. If a coworker was reluctant to support the drive because their job already felt so precarious, one journalist-organizer would counter, "If we really are that close to an edge, then we absolutely should be in a union." This argument became more convincing as word spread of the severance that journalists received when unionized digital shops were shuttered. In some campaigns, the voicing of fear was an effective mobilizing tactic. Inviting coworkers to share "more about what you're afraid of," explains a *Los Angeles Times* journalist-organizer,

> turned out to be a kind of a turning point for us, because management wasn't asking those questions. . . . It felt like no one cared about [workers'] families and struggles they were facing to pay for healthcare, being able to afford living in L.A. . . . It was almost therapeutic, I think, just to have someone ask, "tell me what you want to fix about this place, tell me why it's not working for you, and why you don't see a future here."[23]

Apprehensiveness is not always expressed as a fear of managers. One organizer observed a "Stockholm syndrome-orientation to management," where unionizing is understood as "a personal betrayal." Elements of this attitude surfaced in the HuffPost campaign. A journalist-organizer describes a sense that "people owed something to [then editor-in-chief Arianna Huffington] for helping to elevate their careers in media." Journalists at other shops expressed confidence that problems, should they arise, can be worked out with management. Such optimism can mirror social inequalities between media workers. At ThinkProgress, says a journalist-organizer, unionizing "was actually a hard sell for a lot of our colleagues, particularly the ones who had the least to gain, because they were white guys and already paid well." Organizers worked to persuade their coworkers to adopt a systemic perspective, "that their personal relationship with management is not necessarily reflective of their employee relationship to management."

Although many journalists were close to their coworkers before embarking on their drives, an Al Jazeera America organizer says, "you're just never going to have that level of intimacy, where you really understand and empathize with other people's concerns, unless you engage in an organizing process." This intimacy was semi-publicly performed in a ritual that featured in several drives—the go-around. As a Thrillist organizer says:

> I think that was one of the first times that people who weren't on the organizing committee could really see the strength of what we were

doing. When you're faced with a room with 70 other people who are all going around, talking about their reason for why they want to unionize, or even if they're not certain but they were curious and interested, it was wild. . . . That commiseration was also helpful for a lot of people to hear that everybody is experiencing some facet of the same problem.

In journalists' group meetings, persuasion becomes a collective act. "It was other employees who convinced me," says one journalist. "It was sharing work experience and . . . realizing that everyone sort of felt this uneasiness." Commiserating generates a sense of unity, a vital affective resource to maintain resolve in the face of challenges during a campaign, such as layoffs. And enthusiasm for organizing can be fueled by a sense of possibility, or, as one journalist-organizer puts it, co-creating a "vision for the newsroom we wanted, the place where we wanted to work."

In organizing, worker-to-worker communication is about facilitating contexts for the emergence of solidarities. One journalist says the mobilization process helped colleagues feel "more connected to their coworkers and their actual workplace." Another uses the term "bonding" to summarize the core of their organizing experience. Getting to know coworkers is a dimension of counteracting journalists' alienation from each other, an important part of which is developing awareness of inequalities within a media workforce. A journalist-organizer who describes himself as "a 29-year-old white dude in New York," says that by talking with his colleagues, he "learned a lot about the issues that remote people deal with and the issues that people of color and women deal with, and how those variables can affect one's willingness to ask for a raise or one's willingness to demand transparency from a boss."

Solidarity has also developed, and competition curtailed, between journalists at different shops. Early in campaigns, staff organizers connect journalists with media union members who have already organized their newsrooms, collectively bargained, or worked under a contract. From demystifying steps in a union drive to providing evidence of gains to show unionizing is worthwhile, insight from peers who successfully organized "assuaged a lot of fears," says a Thrillist journalist. These meetings can be transnational. When Vice Canada journalists reached an impasse with card signing, CMG organizers facilitated a Skype strategy session with Vice US and UK counterparts, which "injected life back into the organizing process," says a journalist-organizer. Staff organizers also foster cross-shop solidarity via outreach events such as meet-ups, happy hours, parent-union organizing committees, and maintaining contact with previous inside organizers and bargaining-team members. By 2018, just a few years into the wave, McRobert told us, "we have relationships and networks of trust and solidarity that didn't exist in the industry two and a half years ago."

Within individual shops, mobilization efforts relied on what social movement and industrial relations scholars refer to as "collective action frames."[24] These meaning-making devices, write Peter Gahan and Andreas Pekarek, "not only work to highlight the features of a social situation in a way that elicits a sense of grievance, but also function as modes of articulating strategy."[25] Especially significant for mobilizing union supporters is "motivational (action) framing," which "seeks to translate [rationales for collective organizing] into individual-level participation through socially constructed 'vocabularies of motive,' which are used to provide a compelling account for engaging and sustaining participation."[26]

Three "vocabularies of motive" have been heard across the digital media drives. First: raising standards. This flexible frame accommodates multiple workplace grievances, from lack of diversity to low pay. As organizing victories accumulate, the raising-standards frame is expressed as an industry-wide aspiration. So, collective action frames are not limited to positioning grievances as "sources of injustice"[27]; they also begin to answer the question, "organizing for what?"[28] This is evident in the second frame, too: workplace voice. Without access to a union, there was "no way to say (to management), 'hey, this is important to us, and here's why,'" says one journalist-organizer. In the voice frame, the union is presented as a communication channel through which media workers can affect the setting in which their labor is performed and governed. A third frame is self-determination, which was expressed in organizing phrases like "we are the union" and "the union is us."

Going (very) public

A decisive step in journalists' organizing process is telling management they are unionizing. "We tried for a long time to keep [our drive] under wraps from management because we didn't want them to know about it until we felt like we had some power in numbers," says a journalist-organizer. In theory, critical mass reduces the threat of union busting. Still, campaigns have had different levels of worker support by the time bosses were alerted. Super-majorities are commonplace. We were told, for example, that MTV News organizers had nearly 90 percent support. Other drives had less buy-in when they were announced. A journalist-organizer at Vox admits, "a . . . significant minority of people . . . were probably surprised on the day we went public."

Sometimes journalists can't control when managers are informed. Some drives have been leaked; other times, journalists' strategic missteps can spill the news. During the one-on-one stage, for example, a journalist-organizer says he "started talking to editors higher and higher up the chain," until one editor's reaction made it obvious that "the horses were out of the barn"—the drive had been effectively leaked to management. When journalists do manage to keep a drive quiet until they are ready to go public, common practice is to announce the union and request recognition via a collectively signed letter delivered in (or followed by) a meeting between a group of journalists and management representatives. To avoid singling out individual workers for reprisal, unions are announced collectively. Still, says one journalist, "telling our editor-in-chief the morning that we went public was terrifying."

Employers are hardly expected to welcome a union bid, so journalists shift communication strategies from secrecy to publicity when campaigns are announced. Embracing visibility as a strategic resource to support the drives, unions launch dedicated campaign websites, inside organizers give media interviews, and journalists actively promote and explain their desire to unionize on social media, especially on journalists' favored platform, Twitter. After their campaigns go public, journalist-organizers want to maintain their coworkers' enthusiasm about unionizing, particularly if a union election could be on the horizon. Primarily, however, they use social media to mobilize external publics, namely industry colleagues and followers, and to collectively engage their employer.

As drives go public, one of the unique symbolic traits of new media unions becomes apparent. Rather than name them "Local 123" of a parent union, for example, journalists brand their unions by publication—Mic Union, Vox Media Union, New Yorker Union, and so on. Such outlet-based union identities, says a journalist-organizer, show that media workers "have pride in where they work." But this branding method also brings strategic advantages to campaigns once they move into public media space. "A huge part of our strategy has been leveraging public perception of these progressive brands," says McRobert. "[B]y identifying HuffPost, Vox, and Slate, people know what we're talking about immediately, making it a lot easier to target the institutions."

Going public tends to coincide with heightened rank-and-file participation in campaign communication. "I've had to unlearn some of my professional union organizer training," admits McRobert, referring to union staff keeping a tight grip on public communication. "But honestly," she says, "good luck telling 1,000 journalists that they're not allowed to talk to their peers; they'll just start ignoring you." Early in the wave, organizers' tolerance of journalists' self-determination was put to the test. Union organizers winced when Gawker Media staff wanted to take the unprecedented step of inviting all prospective members of the bargaining unit to publicly express, via comments on a blog post, how they were voting on the union.[29] Union staff were worried—"you don't want the anti-union people to get that platform," one tells us—but knew this was "a very strong-willed group of people, and they were going to do it no matter what, so we just had to sit there and take it." While the public poll has been chalked up as a logical outcome of Gawker's transparency ethos, management was on board. "I thought this would be healthy for the union drive and it would also just be a good thing," says a former editor. "The fact that we were unionizing was a really big story, and I wanted to own our own story instead of letting somebody else do a 'Gawker's unionizing. Here's how they feel internally' [piece]. Like, why not just do it ourselves?"

By taking ownership of communicative aspects of their drives, journalists have prompted union staff to reflect on "where, frankly, decentralizing the paid organizer is really essential," says McRobert. It's essential to not micromanage journalists' social media use in a campaign's post-announcement phase to reinforce that the union is "not a third party," says another organizer. Welcoming journalists' voices is also strategic. These workers' power to affect organizing outcomes lies in their professionally honed communication capacities: journalists' writing skills, self-brands, and social media followers are organizing resources that enable them to summon a public gaze on their employer and solicit support beyond the bounds of their newsroom. Retweeted union posts and messages of solidarity from progressive luminaries—Bernie Sanders tweeted a note of support in the run-up to the Vice Canada vote, for example—won't guarantee a drive's success. Yet expressions of solidarity on social media have been vital in affective organizing in digital journalism: they energize campaigns, generate bonds, and reaffirm journalists' convictions at a moment of uncertainty in the organizing process. Will the employer voluntarily recognize the union? Will management put up a fight? And if the drive goes to a ballot, will a majority of staff vote in favor of unionization?

Mediated solidarities help to sustain the affective work of organizing, with journalists acknowledging how "emotionally exhausting" their drives were. Looking back on their experience, however, inside committee members invoke organizing's intrinsic satisfactions. "[I]t was the most fulfilled I have felt in my four or five years in the workforce as a professional," says a journalist who organized at Vox. Highlighting the collective nature of such fulfillment, journalist-organizers speak of how workplace "morale" is enriched through the mobilization process. "Starting to talk to more employees about how we were feeling about work, and feeling like we were making change, made me so much more engaged," says a journalist-organizer. "I feel so much more empowered and engaged with my colleagues. I feel like I am finally doing something that matters." Such sensations rest upon belief in collective action. In many shops, the durability of the social bonds and the communicative networks cultivated through the process of mobilization are put to the test in the struggles to come in the next moment in the organizing process, recognition.

Notes

1　Cited in Lydia DePillis, "Why Internet Journalists Don't Unionize," *The Washington Post*, January 30, 2015, www.washingtonpost.com/news/storyline/wp/2015/01/30/why-internet-journalists-dont-organize.

2　Lane Windham, "This Is Your Daughter's Labor Movement," *Portside*, June 28, 2018, https://portside.org/2018-06-28/your-daughters-labor-movement.

3　Cited in Jacquie Lee, "Union Activists Take Notice of Workers' Twitter Savvy," *Bloomberg Law*, January 30, 2018, https://news.bloomberglaw.com/daily-labor-report/union-activists-take-notice-of-workers-twitter-savvy.

4　Jane Holgate, Melanie Simms, and Maite Tapia, "The Limitations of the Theory and Practice of Mobilization in Trade Union Organizing," *Economic and Industrial Democracy* 39, no. 4 (2018): 599–616.

5　Jane McAlevey, *No Shortcuts: Organizing for Power in the New Gilded Age* (Oxford: Oxford University Press, 2016), 10.

6　See Melanie Simms and Jane Holgate, "Organising for What? Where Is the Debate on the Politics of Organising?," *Work, Employment and Society* 24, no. 1 (2010): 157–68.

7　Kate Hardy and Katie Cruz, "Affective Organizing: Collectivizing Informal Sex Workers in an Intimate Union," *American Behavioral Scientist* 63, no. 2 (2019): 246.

8　Brian Massumi, *Politics of Affect* (Cambridge: Polity Press, 2015).

9　Caroline Murphy, "Fear and Leadership in Union Organizing Campaigns: An Examination of Workplace Activist Behavior," *Journal of Workplace Rights* (January–March, 2016), https://doi.org/10.1177/2158244015623932.

10　Gregory J. Seigworth and Melissa Gregg, "An Inventory of Shimmers," in *The Affect Theory Reader*, eds. Melissa Gregg and Gregory J. Seigworth (Durham: Duke University Press, 2010), 1.

11　Phoebe Moore, "Tracking Affective Labour for Agility in the Quantified Workplace," *Body & Society* 24, no. 3 (2018): 48.

12　Hardy and Cruz, "Affective Organizing."

13　Rick Fantasia, *Cultures of Solidarity: Consciousness, Action, and Contemporary American Workers* (Berkeley: University of California Press, 1988).

14　Rosemary Hennessy, "Open Secrets: The Affective Cultures of Organizing on Mexico's Northern Border," *Feminist Theory* 10, no. 3 (2009): 310.

15　Raymond Williams, *Culture and Materialism: Selected Essays* (London: Verso, 1980), 50–66.

16　See Dennis Schoeneborn, Timothy R. Kuhn, and Dan Kärreman, "The Communicative Constitution of Organization, Organizing, and Organizationality," *Organization Studies* 40, no. 4 (2019): 475–96.

17　Peter Gahan and Andreas Pekarek, "Social Movement Theory, Collective Action Frames and Union Theory: A Critique and Extension," *British Journal of Industrial Relations* 51, no. 4 (2013): 754–76.

18　Nicole S. Cohen and Greig de Peuter, "Write, Post, Unionize: Journalists and Self-Organization," *Notes from Below* 7 (June 8, 2019), https://notesfrombelow.org/article/write-post-unionize.

19 See Gilles Deleuze, *Spinoza: Practical Philosophy* (San Francisco: City Lights Books, 1998).

20 Melissa Gregg, "On Friday Night Drinks: Workplace Affects in the Age of the Cubicle," in *The Affect Theory Reader*, eds. Melissa Gregg and Gregory J. Seigworth (Durham: Duke University Press, 2010), 267.

21 Micah Uetricht and Barry Eidlin, "U.S. Union Revitalization and the Missing 'Militant Minority'," *Labor Studies Journal* 44, no. 1 (2019): 36–59.

22 Jonathan Lepie, "Is There a Winning Formula for Union Organizing?," *Employee Rights and Responsibilities Journal* 26, no. 2 (2014): 137–52.

23 Labor Video Project, "Democracy Depends on Journalism, Journalism Depends on the Union: Digital Media Workers Speak Out," panel at Labor Notes conference, Chicago, April 17, 2018, www.youtube.com/watch?v=wAaoIjjPRto.

24 Sidney Tarrow, "Mentalities, Political Cultures, and Collective Action Frames: Constructing Meanings through Action," in *Frontiers in Social Movement Theory*, eds. Aldon D. Morris and Carol McClurg Mueller (New Haven: Yale University Press, 1992), 174–202.

25 Gahan and Pekarek, "Social Movement Theory, Collective Action Frames and Union Theory," 762.

26 Gahan and Petarek, "Social Movement Theory, Collective Action Frames and Union Theory," 763.

27 Gahan and Pekarek, "Social Movement Theory, Collective Action Frames and Union Theory," 757.

28 Simms and Holgate, "Organising for What? Where Is the Debate on the Politics of Organising?" 157–68.

29 Revati Prasad, "An Organized Workforce Is Part of Growing Up: Gawker and the Case for Unionizing Digital Newsrooms," *Communication, Culture & Critique* (March 2019), https://doi.org/10.1093/ccc/tcz008.

4 Recognition

Let's get this recognition

In January 2017, MTV News workers were ready to take their union drive public. They had organized for months, secretly meeting in coffee shops and holding pizza parties, gathered to sign union cards in the WGAE's conference room, and, in what has become standard practice in digital media drives, prepared a public statement outlining their intent to unionize. The letter typifies the "Why We Are Organizing" genre. It emphasizes that journalists love their work, champions a union as the best way to ensure worker protection and company success, then lists specific issues workers want to address. At MTV, issues included benefits for permalancers; editorial transparency and protection; a commitment to hiring and advancing workers of color; and guidelines for salaries and severance.[1] Before going public, three workers went to MTV's podcast studio, the only soundproof room in the building, to call their boss. They told him they were unionizing and gave him until the next morning to inform Viacom, which owns MTV. "I was so nervous," one of those workers says about making that call. "I wore my sneakers because I felt my new shoes were too heavy. I felt I couldn't wear any more weight on my ankles; it was extremely intense."

Under US labor law, workers who want to unionize must first approach their employer to request recognition. If workers can show majority support, either through signed authorization cards or other evidence, employers may voluntarily recognize the union. Usually management and union reps hold meetings to work out the details of recognition, such as which workers will be included in the bargaining unit. Sometimes the union can pressure management into an online election run by a third-party site. If employers outright refuse to recognize, the union can petition the NLRB for a certification vote. (In Canada, unions typically file for a certification vote with a provincial or federal labor board as soon as they have enough cards signed.) Once a union is recognized or certified, collective bargaining for a first contract can begin (members don't pay dues until a contract is ratified).

In many newsrooms, recognition has been a relatively smooth process. Once enough cards are signed or names collected, workers draft a public statement, create a union website, launch social media accounts, orchestrate sympathetic media coverage, and formally request unionization in a way that demonstrates strong support, such as hand-delivering a signed letter to management. Once public, announcements are picked up on social media and amplified by other unionized newsrooms and supporters, so unions going public become news events with expressions of solidarity via retweets, likes, and emoji-filled notes of support. This publicity-centered strategy aims to show management unity, both within the newsroom and across the sector, and helps the recognition bid.

Mostly, this strategy has worked. Viacom recognized the MTV News union in two weeks. Gawker Media CEO Nick Denton quipped that he was "intensely relaxed" about his staff's intent to unionize and asked for an online vote mostly for publicity's sake.[2] *The New Republic* management not only recognized the union in a week; it proposed expanding the bargaining unit to include the entire company, "including publishing, marketing, sales, administrative, print, and maintenance teams."[3] "I didn't realize until later, after talking to organizers . . . how atypical our experience had been, to just send an email and they're like, 'oh, OK,'" says a Vice US journalist-organizer of the roughly week-long wait for recognition. Other shops won recognition through a vote, either run online by a third party or supervised by the NLRB.

But recognition is not just a phase for announcing union formation and lodging a formal request. Recognition is also the point when a union campaign can become antagonistic, a reminder that unionization is, ultimately, about confronting class relations. Several companies launched aggressive anti-union campaigns, or "conscious, deliberate" attempts to prevent and undermine union organization.[4] The term anti-unionism encapsulates specific tactics, but is also a "distinct ideological mindset" set on maintaining power relations integral to capitalist employment relationships.[5] Worker collective organization, no matter how positively framed, as most digital media drives have been, are efforts to disrupt employers' monopoly over the ability to "determine the terms and conditions under which workers are employed and work,"[6] which does not typically align with management's interests.

To understand recognition as both a moment in the organizing process and a struggle around worker self-determination, this chapter examines anti-union campaigns at digital outlets and how workers have managed to win recognition at almost every outlet that has sought to unionize. We continue to pay particular attention to the role of affect and communication, which produce relations of solidarity and friendship via public campaigns for recognition as drives transition into struggles with management. Recognition has required that organizers shift communication strategies from inward-focused activities to outward-facing expressions of solidarity and support aimed at fostering "cultures of solidarity."[7]

This strategy has made the digital media union movement exceptionally public, distinguishing it from typical union drives, which don't, for example, provide real-time social media updates on meetings with management: "Let's get this recognition," tweeted Vice UK workers, alongside a photo of four young, stylishly dressed workers standing under a neon Vice logo.[8] Such communication strategies demonstrate how digital media workers are turning the communicative capacities required to generate value for their employers toward pressuring management for recognition. This is a highly strategic way to win union recognition in an industry where public perception is vital for media companies' success. Even when some employer actions—such as shutting down a company, as we discuss later—would typically chill organizing activities,[9] management anti-unionism has bolstered journalists' organizing drives. Workers have won all union drives since 2015, except at Canada's *National Post*. This success rate in the face of active, often threatening, anti-union tactics is unusual, and points to the communicative nature of the struggle for recognition in digital media, both in management strategy and in how journalists fought back.

Union busting

Employer anti-unionism has a long history, and today is supported by a multimillion-dollar "union-avoidance industry."[10] As unionization has spread through media in recent years, companies have taken preventative measures. In 2018, *New York* magazine management hosted a "union-busting meeting" where lawyers advised on a potential union drive, three months before staff announced unionization.[11] That month, Tronc started looking for a director of labor relations, whose job would be "maintaining the non-union status of the unorganized employee population."[12] Earlier that year, law firm Jones Day hosted an invitation-only, day-long session on "labor and employment law in the news media industry," hosting execs from large media outlets like *The New York Times*, *The Washington Post*, and Atlantic Media.[13] As Nolan writes, such tactics are "*de rigeur*" in American anti-union companies," yet "most of those companies do not publish quite so much progressive journalism."[14]

Organizers were surprised by aggressive anti-union campaigns at media outlets whose content is so outwardly progressive. Digital shops, explains a NewsGuild union organizer, "[are] smaller, there's less of a corporate feel to them, they're more open, and they want to have harmonious relationships . . . with their employees." That frequently turned out not to be the case. Management at Slate, Vox, Thrillist, DNAInfo and Gothamist, Vice Canada, Law360, Fusion, and other digital outlets and newspapers ran anti-union campaigns described as "aggressive" and "highly scripted."[15]

The most extreme response came from Joe Ricketts, the conservative billionaire owner of DNAinfo and Gothamist, when the newly merged newsrooms began an organizing drive in April 2017. Organizers say the union bid was not narrowly about compensation, but rather to address issues like the integration of the two newsrooms and to shape how jobs would be defined. Yet Ricketts wrote to staff, "As long as it's my money that's paying for everything, I intend to be the one making the decisions about the direction of the business."[16] During the drive, staff were threatened in "coded and explicit ways" via group and one-on-one meetings: a reporter told the *New Yorker* that she was brought into a room with management, alone, and told "explicitly that, if the union was successful, Ricketts would close the company rather than recognize" the union.[17] Still, in October, staff voted 25–2 to unionize with the WGAE in an NLRB vote. A week later, Ricketts shuttered the sites, the homepage and archives gone, journalists left jobless and without access to their work.

Typically, employers use two main strategies to fight unionization: union substitution and union suppression.[18] Union substitution aims to make a union seem unnecessary, bolstering workers' loyalty by aligning their interests with employers.[19] Digital media companies excel here, presenting themselves as desirable places to work (see: carefully designed open-concept offices, in-house bars, and other amenities) and relying on the perception of being a cool employer as a labor control strategy.[20] In more active union substitution, companies provide "extras" like free meals, small bonuses, or company swag, or will suddenly offer to settle longstanding complaints once a union drive begins.[21] BuzzFeed's CEO Jonah Peretti, for example, gave his New York staff $250 each in bonuses in 2017 after telling staff that "he doesn't think unionization is right for BuzzFeed."[22]

Several journalists describe promises made—imminent raises, open-door policies—and management stressing "that things are really good" once union drives went public, yet journalists viewed such claims as platitudes. At Vice Canada, for example, management promised to start a diversity committee that, according to one organizer, was led by white people: "All of a sudden, they care about diversity." Another popular tactic is describing the workplace as a family, discourse long deployed by capital to quell labor unrest.[23] Several journalists we interviewed were dismayed by their bosses' use of "family" during union drives. "Most people were like, 'I've never met you. Who are you?'" says a Fusion organizer. "They say that we're all this big family but look what happens when you try to unionize," says a journalist who helped organize non-profit ThinkProgress. "They act like any other management team. It was frustrating." An organizer tells us that some bosses even cried and tried to make members feel guilty, presenting a union drive as a personal attack.

Union suppression is more direct and coercive. Many employers, including Vox, Vice Canada, MTV News, and BuzzFeed, stalled recognition by trying to cut the number of people eligible to be in the bargaining unit. The ability to stall and dissuade workers from unionizing is one reason why employers often request a formal vote and why unions push for quick recognition. Management will argue that workers have managerial or supervisory status, or that they have access to confidential information that could cause a conflict of interest, or, as the Chicago Tribune Guild reported, shift job titles and responsibilities so that "[s]uddenly, an awfully high proportion of our newsroom colleagues are considered 'managers' or 'supervisors.'"[24] One journalist-organizer describes bargaining unit challenges as a "union-busting tactic" designed to scare people from vocalizing union support. His company classified people "pretty low on the totem pole" as managers to keep the numbers of union members down. He points to the problem of fluid job titles and descriptions in digital media: "someone like me, who did have three direct reports, was also spending four-fifths of every day making content. I would argue that . . . even though people report to me, I write, and I research, and I report. I am labor."

Union suppression aims to "plant anti-union seeds of doubt in workers' minds"[25] or "creat[e] an atmosphere of fear and trepidation."[26] Tactics can include disciplining or firing workers who organize and forcing staff to watch anti-union videos, but more common in digital media is management delivering anti-union memos and speeches that repeat well-worn anti-union arguments (many of these, unsurprisingly, were leaked to media). Such texts commonly position digital media workplaces as unique, and digital media workers as *not* workers. Long before the union drive in three BuzzFeed newsrooms launched, Peretti told staff that while "unions have had a positive impact on a lot of places, like if you're working on an assembly line," BuzzFeed is more akin to a "flexible, dynamic" tech company, where there's an "alliance between managers and employees."[27] Similarly, Thrillist CEO Ben Lerer expressed concern about "the effect the union would have on our unique culture."[28] A journalist-organizer who heard Lerer's speech says, "It was another classic example of, 'I support the labor movement, but it's just not right for us.'" Similar rhetoric was deployed to resist the first major effort at unionizing newspapers in the 1930s, when North American publishers, anticipating losing their cheap workforce, claimed it would be "degrading" for journalists to unionize.[29] They spoke of journalism as a profession "too fine to be deadened by the fetishes of maximum and minimum pay."[30] Like today, publishers defused scrutiny of power relations by stressing a common identity between publishers and journalists.

Management communications have painted unions as third parties parachuting in to disrupt unique employer-employee relationships. Slate Group Chairman Jacob Weisberg warned of union-imposed "bureaucracy and procedure" that is "just not Slate-y,"[31] and many newsrooms were told that unionizing could mean losing much-desired flexibility. Union staff warned journalists about the word flexibility. "These days, flexibility no longer means 'you have a laptop; you can work from anywhere,'" says a News-Guild organizer. "It means, 'you have a laptop, so you're gonna go home and finish this at home until 2 a.m.'" But while organizers prepped journalists for a predictable anti-union script, many didn't expect such sentiment from supposedly progressive colleagues. One Slate journalist was surprised by "how deeply anti-union propaganda had penetrated even the supposed smart set."

Many anti-union speeches were delivered at captive audience meetings, typically management's most effective anti-union tool.[32] Captive audience meetings are a specific form of communication: compulsory meetings where workers are forced to listen to the boss's opinions on unionization. While management summons workers under the guise of an "all-hands" or town hall meeting, the term "captive audience" speaks to their coercive nature. Captive audience meetings are a "display of employer power," argues David Doorey, as only management has the capacity to gather workers in one place to force them to listen to ideas with which they may disagree.[33] Journalists who sat through these meetings describe them as "paternalistic" and "very intense." After Vox journalists went public, management scheduled mandatory meetings, to which people away for Thanksgiving were required to call in. "People cried in almost every one of those meetings," says a journalist-organizer. At Law360, which faced an aggressive anti-union campaign, management retained two well-known "union-busting" law firms and held two weeks of group and individual meetings.[34] Twenty-four hours after 90 percent of Fusion editorial workers signed union cards, management flew to New York, Miami, Los Angeles, and Oakland to hold captive audience meetings, where workers were told a "union would harm employee pay and benefits" and general relations with management.[35] As journalists tell it, management messaging in these meetings was textbook: unions were portrayed as a relic, outsiders that would impede companies' flexibility. Staff were told, misleadingly, that unions would lower pay and benefits, and that staff could be fired for not paying dues. Staff at non-profit StoryCorps were called "entitled" for requesting union recognition.[36] A Fusion journalist-organizer reads management's pushback as fear: "The reality is that they do lose out when you get a seat at the table. They do lose out when you do get to demand salary minimums, when you get to demand a minimum for your healthcare, paid leave" she says. "When you're a less exploited worker, your boss loses out, and that's why they're scared of the union."

Ultimately, anti-union campaigns failed. Although management has more power and resources to communicate directly with staff and command attention,[37] journalists took great offense to the scripted nature of management responses. At the *Los Angeles Times*, for example, then-owner Tronc left a seven-page anti-union letter on everyone's desk with generic language that read: "you could be STUCK with the [Union]."[38] And while captive audience meetings and other employer anti-union tactics have historically been successful in a range of sectors,[39] in digital media, they were generally "a disaster for the company's case against the union," according to a journalist-organizer. "They made this whole pitch about how we were such a close-knit family and that the union would separate us, and we were like, 'we're seeing you for the first time in this calendar year.' I don't even know this guy's last name, and you're saying that [the union] is going to damage our relationship?"

Union organizers, on the other hand, were able to predict management's moves, which helped build trust between the union and journalists. A News-Guild organizer explains why captive audience meetings at Law360, run by company-hired consultants, backfired:

> There was no nuance. The consultants didn't actually learn anything about these journalists and what they do. . . . As a matter of their profession, [journalists are] critical thinkers. They investigate, they analyze, they research. To have an outside expert come in and try to tell them what they should be thinking—journalists didn't take kindly to that.

She says captive audience meetings encouraged people "on the fence" to sign union cards.

Organizers countered anti-union campaigns by drawing on longstanding organizing principles, including maintaining a focus on the issues and generating sympathetic public support.[40] A self-organizing strategy has been crucial for winning recognition amid anti-union campaigns. While the specificities of digital media drives vary, common among them is that journalists themselves initiate and drive unionization: the decision to unionize comes from inside newsrooms and journalists are core inside organizers. This strategy, supported by both the WGAE and the NewsGuild in a model of "worker-driven but staff-facilitated" organizing, inoculates journalists from management's claim that a union is an infiltrating third party.[41] Journalists embrace the notion that "we are the union," and the entire mobilization and recognition process, including going public, emphasizes that the union "is made up of [journalists'] colleagues and directed by them." Organizers harness this sentiment and strategically use communication strategies to build solidarity and counter management anti-unionism.

Putting the pressure on

During the recognition phase, management communications aim to instill fear in workers (a union means sacrificing flexibility for no guarantee of higher pay), stress division (the union is a third party that will come between us), and placate workers (give us another chance, and we'll give you what you want). The mode is coercive and intimidating, but also superficial and patronizing. Organizers pitch their responses at a more positive register, emphasizing solidarity, care, and collective power. From wearing union buttons at meetings to "walking out" to eat lunch together in a visible spot in the newsroom, workers' recognition strategies aim to build cultures of solidarity, or space to experience "the values, practices, and institutional manifestations of mutuality."[42]

Workers counter management anti-unionism with communication for collective care. Immediately following management memos or captive audience meetings, inside organizing committees create space to address colleagues' concerns. "Just touching base with everyone and making sure everyone's OK," explains a journalist-organizer. "That was a lot of [the] work." Through group and one-on-one conversations, as well as dedicated union Slack channels, organizers maintain emphasis on the issues that originally sparked unionization and supportively respond to fears or confusion arising from management response. Rather than engaging in ideological battles, they tend to focus on technical and factual claims. One committee recorded the CEO's speech and annotated it for circulation: "we . . . pulled out the classic union-busting lines and debunked them," says a journalist-organizer. Several committees launched websites to counter general anti-union claims via extensive FAQ sections, preemptively dispelling their bosses' union-busting myths. "If the contract doesn't improve our salaries, benefits and working conditions enough to justify the dues, we can, and will vote it down," notes Law360's online "Union Busting Playbook." "WE negotiate our contract, and decide what we want and need" (Law360 Guild).[43] Such actions emphasize that workers care about each other and hold similar values, and present a union as a collective structure for long-term support.

Other responses are more public. After a captive audience meeting at Fusion, the organizing committee held its own meeting in the form of a union-sponsored pizza lunch. "The mood of our meeting couldn't have been more different [than the captive audience meetings]," says an organizer. "It was just like we had a little party in the middle of the day, and it was a very lighthearted atmosphere." Several newsrooms have organized pizza lunches where everyone wears union T-shirts, a visible display of support management is sure to notice. Gatherings include happy hours and lunches near the office, doubly conceived as spaces to answer questions and publicly demonstrate united support for union recognition. Two months after requesting recognition, BuzzFeed News union members held birthday parties in four different offices with balloons and cake, whose icing read "recognize our union." While the act of gathering to celebrate to demand recognition keeps within journalists' comfort zones—most want to stay on good terms with their managers—such actions also reflect an ethic of affective, or "passionate" organizing in new media union drives,[44] which is as much about building community and relationships as improving working conditions (although workers have also escalated to more confrontational tactics, such as writing letters, tweeting at management, and threatening to walk out to win recognition). "My main argument for unionism in journalism is the same as anywhere," says a journalist-organizer. "You actually get to know your co-workers in a profound way, which you would never, ever have if you didn't organize." Generating such "associational bonds"[45] has been a vital force for building capacity to secure recognition and, as we show in Chapter 5, eventually negotiate strong contracts.

Organizers intensify pressure on management by orienting digital media workers' professional skills and capacities toward winning recognition. In some cases, workers went on a Slack strike, a form of work stoppage where workers simultaneously log off the internal chat program to which they're perpetually plugged in. In an email to staff, Vox organizers explained: "Set yourself to away and mute your notifications for one hour, and change your status to include the voxunion emoji. . . . Given how much time we all spend in Slack, this is kind of like holding up a sign. Digital media!"[46] To a traditional union organizer, the tactic might sound "absurd," says a journalist-organizer. But "in a digital media newsroom, everyone going dark on Slack . . . something is going on. That's wild." The action points to the vitality of digital media workers' communicative capacities, which when silenced, make visible their potential.

As expected, social media has been a key site of digital media union communications, especially during recognition campaigns. After going public, shops set up a Twitter account, and journalists change their avatars to union logos and fill their streams with updates about the union, aimed at building public and industry support and getting their bosses' attention. The tone is generally positive, playful, and image heavy. These are not exclusively hashtag campaigns (although hashtags are used, such as *New York* magazine's #NYMagUnionBecause tag), but rather dedicated channels for amplifying union drives aimed squarely at winning recognition and, later, bargaining strong contracts. Content is very on-brand: pets regularly feature, as do selfies displaying union buttons and clever plays on popular memes. Pitchfork workers curated a Spotify playlist of "union, labor and collectivism-related jams" called "Hammer and Sickle" while waiting to be recognized. The BuzzFeed News Union tweeted a tally of the number of days it took for many unionized newsrooms to be recognized: "This week we hit our 56th day without recognition . . . our analysis found it took similar outlets an average of 21 days to be voluntarily recognized."[47]

A particularly effective strategy has been drawing attention to the hypocrisy of image-conscious media companies claiming a progressive or pro-labor stance, yet refusing to recognize their own staffs' union. "It was the most hypocritical thing on the planet," says one journalist-organizer of companies that initially refused to recognize. Another says that such double standards have "exposed" media companies and made them "susceptible to bad PR more so than other industries," which has helped win recognition. Journalists have promoted labor-friendly articles companies have published and tweeted directly at ostensibly progressive media owners to recognize their employees' unions. "It's kind of a smear campaign in a way," says a journalist-organizer. "It's not necessarily intended to be negative, but it's certainly intended to put the pressure on, and make sure that everybody's watching to see what this company's going to do and if it's going to live up to the values that it preaches." She thinks media companies are "uniquely vulnerable to these kinds of pressure campaigns." Thrillist workers and supporters, for example, tweeted directly at Lerer until he recognized the union. Thrillist's "entire strategy as a company depends on the viability of [Lerer's] name," says a journalist-organizer. "These are people with images they have to uphold," says another. "They're public figures, they donate to the Hillary Clinton campaign . . . they want to be recognized as benevolent Democrats."

Journalists use Twitter to provide real-time updates and streams of solidarity messages for other shops to build sector-wide support. Organizers say such orchestrated expressions of solidarity put a positive spin on unionizing, which encouraged media managers to recognize unions. What helped his newsroom win, says a journalist-organizer, was "internal pressure and enthusiasm, and that there were public displays of camaraderie and willingness to help each other and giving a positive face to it, that 'we're not here necessarily to fight your management, we are here to help each other.'" Their approach reflects an ethos of "radical transparency" (many people tweet how they're going to vote in union elections, a decision usually kept secret during drives) and general comfort being online, as well as digital media workers' privileged position in the communications infrastructure. Journalists could, with relative ease, ask other media outlets to write about their campaigns or tweet clever, captivating content that built general support, contributing to an unprecedented level of publicity around new media union drives compared to other labor struggles.

Digital media workers are "extremely online people," says a journalist. And in many ways, it's been easy for journalists and organizing committees to strategically use social media to pressure employers, which has been a distinct advantage in this sector and one reason why so many shops have been recognized quickly. "The majority of times [employers] have thought twice about holding these all-hands meetings where they tell everybody what a bad idea it is to organize, because they know that it's gonna be on Twitter within minutes," says a NewsGuild organizer. "It's a huge piece of leverage. . . . Instead of having to spend months and months bogged down in an anti-union campaign, we can really focus that energy and attention on organizing around the issues, and getting prepared for contract negotiations."

Communication is a source of power for digital media workers, particularly when they turn the communicative capacities integral to their work creating value for media companies toward more politicized ends. Says a journalist-organizer:

> We're not workers who, when we go on strike, we can turn the lights off. But we can make a lot of noise and make a lot of people angry really easily, and we have a responsibility to do that. Not just to benefit our colleagues in journalism, but any workers that can benefit from that. I think that's where a lot of the power comes from in this sector and I'm encouraged to see people using that power.

Unionizing is the status quo

In April 2019, seven weeks after requesting recognition, members of the BuzzFeed News Union posted a thread to Twitter. "We came to the table today ready to meet with BuzzFeed execs about finally recognizing our union," they write.[48] "Five minutes after the meeting was scheduled to start, they told us they weren't going to show up." They accuse management of "engaging in clear union-busting" by refusing to recognize the entire newsroom as an editorial unit and whittling down the list of potential unit members based on job titles, a strategy of weakening the union before it's even certified. "Unionizing is increasingly the status quo for our industry," the thread concludes. "But BuzzFeed is choosing a path of avoidance and delays. It does not have to be this way." The thread, retweeted and liked thousands of times, encapsulates the process of recognition we've described in this chapter. As digital media companies use age-old tactics to avoid unionization, digital media workers respond by harnessing their strategic position in the means of communication to win recognition, reorienting their communicative capacities from generating value through commodity production toward building solidarity on an expanded terrain. After five months and a boisterous staff walkout, BuzzFeed recognized the union, which was certified through a third-party card check in July 2019.

Cultures of solidarity, argues Fantasia, emerge when workers "rely on their mutual solidarity as the basis for their power."[49] Our analysis of the mobilization and recognition phases of digital media unionization reflects this process. Generating solidarity as a response to management anti-unionism has been vital in securing recognition and establishing strong digital media unions. Journalists' actions and efforts to win recognition are as much about convincing management to recognize as demonstrating what workers can accomplish if they have each other's backs. "It was awesome," says Amanda Holpuch, who helped organize The Guardian US. "It was a really positive process." She sensed that their boss was supportive, because it was clear that the union drive "was really bringing together the staff as a whole and [that] we were all working towards something together." Another important dynamic, says a WGAE organizer, is that editorial management often aligns with union members against corporate management, especially on issues such as editorial independence or improved parental leave. So, while union organizing is typically a form of disruption, to use a well-loved industry term, as it tempers management's unilateral power and democratizes the workplace, unionization in digital media has not been framed as such. Workers and organizers frame drives positively, as an optimistic mode of collective expression and support for something better than what currently exists.

Much of this solidarity and its expressions have emerged because of management opposition. "The more there are anti-union campaigns, and the more that [journalists] have to fight to unionize in the first place, that builds up a sense of consciousness," says a journalist-organizer. "When [journalists] get on the other side of that, they are much more class-conscious." Unionizing helped digital journalists develop an understanding of labor-capital relations that may have not been clear before. Another journalist-organizer says:

There's this really successful and well-funded campaign that's been going for decades now in the United States that's been trying to systematically dismantle labor and to basically . . . demonize unions. Some people have passively absorbed that narrative for most of their adult life, and then all of a sudden, they're being confronted with, "oh shit, my boss is fighting me really hard on this," because actually fairness and basic workplace democracy is not natural or inherent to every workplace, which is why a boss would be so freaked out that you would want to bring it to your workplace. So, it sounds silly, but [unionizing] is like a consciousness-raising moment. It's a learning thing.

While for all but a few digital newsrooms the recognition process has led to victory, for most journalists, winning union certification is just the start. While the mobilization and recognition phases enact solidarity and class consciousness, and while winning a vote or voluntary recognition is exhilarating after months (or years) of work, it's during the next phase, contract negotiations, when employers escalate their opposition. Winning a vote "was very exciting," says journalist Gregg Levine, who helped organize Al-Jazeera America. "But like with any election, it's not the last day of your struggle. It's the first." As newly certified unions began to bargain their first contracts, they encountered lawyers and expert negotiators, what one journalist calls "the sharper end of management." It's to negotiation that we now turn.

Notes

1 The MTV News Unionizing Committee, "Why We're Organizing," *Writers Guild of America, East*, accessed October 9, 2019, digitalwritersunion.org/mtv.

2 Peter Sterne, "Nick Denton 'Intensely Relaxed' by Gawker's Union Drive," *Politico*, April 16, 2015, www.politico.com/media/story/2015/04/nick-denton-intensely-relaxed-by-gawkers-union-drive-003863.

3 The New Republic, "*The New Republic*'s Leadership Advances Proposal for Unionization of All Staff," *The New Republic*, April 18, 2018, https://newrepublic.com/article/148041/new-republics-leadership-advances-proposal-unionization-staff.

4 Tony Dundon and Gregor Gall, "Anti-Unionism: Contextual and Thematic Issues," in *Global Anti-Unionism: Nature, Dynamics, Trajectories and Outcomes*, eds. Gregor Gall and Tony Dundon (London: Palgrave Macmillan, 2013), 1.

5 Dundon and Gall, "Anti-Unionism," 3.

6 Dundon and Gall, "Anti-Unionism," 3.

7 Rick Fantasia, *Cultures of Solidarity: Consciousness, Action, and Contemporary American Workers* (Berkeley: University of California Press, 1988).

8 VICE UK UNION (@VICEUKUNION), "Excited to go into our next meeting with management," tweet, April 24, 2019, https://twitter.com/VICEUKUNION/status/1121051186986201089.

9 Stephanie Ross and Larry Savage, "An Introduction to Anti-Unionism in Canada," in *Labour under Attack: Anti-Unionism in Canada*, eds. Stephanie Ross and Larry Savage (Halifax and Winnipeg: Fernwood, 2018), 11.

10 Ross and Savage, "An Introduction to Anti-Unionism in Canada," 13.

11 Hamilton Nolan, "New York Magazine Hosts Union-Busting Meeting," *Splinter*, September 6, 2018, https://splinternews.com/new-york-magazine-hosts-union-busting-meeting-1828841682.

12 Keith J. Kelly, "Tronc Is Looking for New Head of Labor Relations," *New York Post*, September 18, 2018, https://nypost.com/2018/09/18/tronc-looking-for-new-head-of-labor-relations/.

13 Andrew McCormick, "A Law Firm in the Trenches against Media Unions," *Columbia Journalism Review*, December 13, 2018, www.cjr.org/analysis/jones-day-unions-slate-strike.php.

14 Nolan, "New York Magazine Hosts Union-Busting Meeting," 2018.

15 Stephanie Russell-Kraft, "The Aggressive Anti-Union Campaign at Story Corps," *The Nation*, July 17, 2017, www.thenation.com/article/the-aggressive-anti-union-campaign-at-storycorps/; Kristina Bui and Nastaran Mohit, "After 136 Years, L.A. Times Journalists Win Their Union," *Labor Notes*, March 1, 2018, www.labornotes.org/2018/03/after-136-years-la-times-journalists-win-their-union.

16 Andy Newman, "Gothamist and DNAinfo Newsrooms Now Have a Union," *The New York Times*, October 27, 2017, www.nytimes.com/2017/10/27/nyregion/dnainfo-gothamist-union.html.

17 Anna Heyward, "The Story Behind the Unjust Shutdown of Gothamist and DNAInfo," *The New Yorker*, November 14, 2017, www.newyorker.com/culture/culture-desk/the-story-behind-the-unjust-shutdown-of-gothamist-and-dnainfo.

18 Gregor Gall, "Employer Opposition to Union Recognition," in *Union Organizing: Campaigning for Trade Union Recognition*, ed. Gregor Gall (London: Routledge, 2003), 81.

19 Gall, "Employer Opposition to Union Recognition," 88; Savage and Ross, "An Introduction to Anti-Unionism in Canada," 13.

20 Nicole S. Cohen and Greig de Peuter, "'I Work at VICE Canada and I Need a Union': Organizing Digital Media," in *Labour under Attack: Anti-Unionism in Canada*, eds. Stephanie Ross and Larry Savage (Halifax and Winnipeg: Fernwood, 2018), 114–28.

21 Savage and Ross, "An Introduction to Anti-Unionism in Canada," 13; Gall, "Employer Opposition to Union Recognition."

22 Molly Osberg, "BuzzFeed London: Layoffs Coming, Unions Busten, Christmas Cancelled, But Free Caviar," *Splinter*, December 22, 2017, https://splinternews.com/buzzfeed-london-layoffs-coming-unions-busted-christm-1821532976.

23 Jane Sangster, "The Softball Solution: Female Workers, Male Managers, and the Operation of Paternalism at Westclox, 1923–60," *Labour/Le Travail* 32 (1993): 167–99.

24 Chicago Tribune Guild (@CTGuild), "Good morning! Beautiful day for negotiations, isn't it?," tweet, June 21, 2019, https://twitter.com/CTGuild/status/1142069983721283584.

25 Ross and Savage, "An Introduction to Anti-Unionism in Canada," 14.

26 Gall, "Employer Opposition to Union Recognition," 87.

27 Cora Lewis, "BuzzFeed Founder Jonah Peretti: 'I Don't Think a Union Is Right' for Staff," *BuzzFeed*, August 14, 2015, www.buzzfeednews.com/article/coralewis/buzzfeed-founder-jonah-peretti-i-dont-think-a-union-is-right.

28 Hamilton Nolan, "The Dismal Thrillist Anti-Union Campaign," *The Concourse*, October 3, 2017, https://theconcourse.deadspin.com/the-dismal-thrillist-anti-union-campaign-1793157413.

29 Harry Christian, "Journalists' Occupational Ideologies and Press Commercialisation," in *The Sociology of Journalism and the Press*, ed. Harry Christian, *Sociological Review Monograph* 29 (Staffordshire: University of Keele, 1980), 275.

30 Bonnie Brennen, "The Emergence of Class Consciousness in the American Newspaper Guild," in *Class and News*, ed. Don Heider (Lanham: Rowman & Littlefield, 2004), 237.

31 David Uberti, "Slate's Biggest Enemies Are Donald Trump and Its Staff Trying to Unionize," *Splinter*, March 8, 2017, https://splinternews.com/slates-biggest-enemies-are-donald-trump-and-its-staff-t-1797446734.

32 Sara Slinn, "Captive Audience Meetings and Forced Listening: Lessons for Canada from the American Experience," *Relations Industrielles/Industrial Relations* 63, no. 4 (2008): 694–718.

33 David J. Doorey, "The Medium and the 'Anti-Union' Message: 'Forced Listening' and Captive Audience Meetings in Canadian Labor Law," *Comparative Labor Law and Policy Journal* 29 (2007): 80.

34 Law360 Guild, "The Union Busting Playbook," accessed October 9, 2019, www.law360guild.org/union-busting.

35 Daniel Marans, "Fusion Staff Pressures CEO for Union Recognition," *HuffPost US*, October 24, 2016, www.huffingtonpost.ca/entry/fusion-staff-pressure-ceo-for-union-recognition_n_580e69c2e4b02444efa4c7db.

36 Hamilton Nolan, "StoryCorps, of All Places, Is Running and Anti-Union Campaign," *Splinter*, June 27, 2017, https://splinternews.com/storycorps-of-all-places-is-running-an-anti-union-cam-1796429329.

37 Gall, "Employer Opposition to Union Recognition," 79.

38 Tronc's letter is available at https://static1.squarespace.com/static/59f32b4b12abd94fac1a508b/t/59f37468f9619a2518e031b3/1509127278040/union-busting-flyer.pdf, accessed October 15, 2019; see also Alex Press, "I've Got Your Back, and You've Got Mine," *Jacobin*, October 28, 2017, www.jacobinmag.com/2017/10/los-angeles-times-union-organizing.

39 Kate Bronfenbrenner, "The Role of Union Strategies in NLRB Certification Elections," *ILR Review* 50, no. 2 (1997): 195–212.

40 Gall, "Employer Opposition to Union Recognition," 90.

41 Nicole S. Cohen and Greig de Peuter, "Write, Post, Unionize: Journalists and Self-Organization," *Notes from Below* 7, 2019, https://notesfrombelow.org/article/write-post-unionize.

42 Fantasia, *Cultures of Solidarity*, 25.

43 Law360 Guild, "The Union Busting Playbook," http://www.law360guild.org/union-busting-playbook.

44 Rosemary Hennessy, "Open Secrets: The Affective Cultures of Organizing on Mexico's Northern Border," *Feminist Theory* 10, no. 3 (2009): 309–22.

45 Fantasia, *Cultures of Solidarity*, 232.

46 Maxwell Tani, "Vox Employees Are Going on a 'Slack Strike' to Push for a Union," *Business Insider*, January 3, 2018, www.businessinsider.com/vox-employees-are-going-on-a-slack-strike-to-push-for-a-union-2018-1.

47 BuzzFeed News Union (@bfnewsunion), "Today marks two months since going public with our campaign to form a union," tweet, April 12, 2019, https://twitter.com/bfnewsunion/status/1116711421096734723.

48 BuzzFeed News Union (@bfnewsunion), "We came to the table today ready to meet with BuzzFeed execs," April 3, 2019, https://twitter.com/bfnewsunion/status/1113529162575355904/photo/1.

49 Fantasia, *Cultures of Solidarity*, 19.

5   Negotiation

Fair contract now!

When the Fast Company Union ratified its first contract in June 2019, the union excitedly tweeted its top gains, including "401k matching!" and "A strong severance plan!"[1] Collective agreements rarely generate buzz, let alone exclamation marks. With industrial-relations jargon, hyper-formality, and a prescriptive tone, the average collective agreement—a legally binding contract that sets out terms and conditions of employment—isn't exactly an exhilarating read. But journalists' first contracts are an artifact of their unions' tenacity, a barometer of their power, and a statement of their vision for the industry. Journalists' collective agreements further illustrate the communicative constitution of organizing: contract language is bargaining's terrain of struggle. The negotiated phrasing of the various articles that constitute a collective agreement produce, in aggregate, the normative framework shaping the material conditions of media labor and governing the power relations of the newsroom.

In their study of collective agreements, union researchers Tom Juravich, Kate Bronfenbrenner, and Robert Hickey ask, "What do these first contracts provide that makes the struggle worthwhile?"[2] In the case of digital media unions, inaugural agreements measure up to the aspirations that initially motivated journalists to organize. In this chapter, we examine the next stage in the process of unionizing: negotiating a first collective agreement. We consider the process of forming bargaining committees and meeting management at the table, a highly participatory process led by journalists themselves and continuing mobilization and communicative practices enacted throughout organizing drives. We then review select contracts bargained to date, and assess their implications for workers and journalism more broadly. We find that overall, collective bargaining agreements (CBAs) have brought long-term standards in journalism to digital newsrooms and have set new standards and raised basic expectations in the industry. Yet they also demonstrate some of the contradictory aspects of unions under capitalism: on the one hand, CBAs codify the power of capital in production by reinforcing management's right to control "enterprise goals and the direction of the work process," but they are also a manifestation of unionized workers' ability to democratically participate in "workplace governance."[3] The stakes are high, and the negotiations that produce CBAs can be fraught. One worker, for example, says it was a "brutal fight" to get her union's first contract. Journalists at the *Los Angeles Times* launched a protest in early September 2019 after 14 months of contract negotiations. After an all-night bargaining session on Labor Day, journalists walked through the newsroom in yellow L.A. Times Guild T-shirts chanting, "Fair contract now!"[4] Indeed, many shops' struggles to win strong contracts pushed them to engage in the most militant actions so far in the digital media union movement, demonstrating that after unions are recognized, class struggle between workers and management unfolds and often intensifies at the bargaining table.

At the table

Bargaining is a long process that begins well before workers and management meet at the table. Once a union is certified or recognized, members or unit leadership elect or appoint people to serve on the bargaining committee. Committee membership is strategic. Needed are diligent and patient people—bargaining can be frustratingly slow—but also representatives from each of a company's verticals and departments, remote workers, women, and people of color. "Most newsrooms are so white that [the bargaining committee] is also typically going to mirror the newsroom, but we encourage women and people of color in leadership roles," says a NewsGuild organizer. Bargaining committees can be large, but are representative and enable more workers to develop leadership skills, which builds union capacity.

Although the thought of negotiating with their bosses can intimidate media workers, many are keen to participate, even those who were initially against the union drive, and especially organizing committee members, who want to finish the work they started. One reporter stepped up because she saw a connection between the labor issues she reported on and the issues her colleagues wanted to address, saying, "Being on the bargaining committee was an opportunity to translate those things that I so frequently write about and care a lot about to an actual document that would enact change."

Bargaining prep is intensive. Committees are trained on collective negotiating and labor law, and workers from other shops visit to share negotiating experiences. Organizers aim to demystify the process ("are we going to be sitting at a table?" "What should I wear?" and "Who will be there?" are some of workers' initial questions) and to emotionally prepare workers to face management. "It's very hard to hear some of the things that you hear at the table," says a WGAE organizer, so workers need to be ready "emotionally and psychologically."

Prep also involves examining other outlets' contracts. While committees can use model union contracts and draw on language from the increasing number of digital media agreements, the aim is to negotiate a contract that is workplace-specific and guided by members' priorities, which are typically gauged through an online survey. Surveys can be long, containing hundreds of questions, but provide crucial insights on workplace experiences. Member-led priority setting has resulted in innovative contract provisions. Vice workers, for example, wanted their second contract to protect workers' rights to use preferred gender pronouns. "At the time, there were no other contracts with this language," says Arsenia Reilly-Collins, WGAE's Director of Contract Campaigns, which meant no pre-existing language to borrow. So, the committee used wording from a member's email about preferred pronouns, which is now Article XXIII in the contract.

Overall, digital media unions enact a democratic and participatory approach to collective bargaining: contracts are not imposed from above in closed-door negotiations, but developed through "open bargaining," a practice that can achieve strong agreements and build union power.[5] In this model, collective agreements are negotiated by workers themselves in an open, transparent way. Members are encouraged to attend bargaining sessions, and committees provide colleagues with frequent updates so that by the time a contract is presented for ratification, members know what's in it (unions will often tweet out portions of the contract before it's ratified, defying traditional labor movement conventions). Committees circulate reports after sessions, and each member has a "buddy list" of people they are in regular contact with during bargaining.

Negotiating a first contract is an exercise in envisioning an ideal workplace, and union staff push workers to think more ambitiously than their instinct may allow. One journalist says her committee's thinking was constrained by existing working conditions. "We were coming from a . . . workplace that really never goes above and beyond in terms of providing for us," she says. Their union rep "was able to convince us . . . that we deserve more than this . . . that we start high and give ourselves enough leverage to bargain back down to a place where we're still comfortable. That was incredibly eye-opening." Bargaining committee members described a range of experiences at the table, including feeling "awkward" and "anxiety ridden." One member found it "satisfying" to confirm what he always thought was a discrepancy between how management purported to treat their employees and how they actually viewed them, saying:

> All the things you suspect about managers and corporate entities, how they behave in the world, how they see . . . their employees . . . you actually see them confirming your suspicions in real time. It's both maddening and kind of satisfying.

At the table, negotiations are formal. Typically, management is represented by an HR person, a business executive, and an editorial manager. Most companies retain a lawyer; many use notoriously anti-union firm Jones Day.[6] For the union, the lead negotiator—WGAE or NewsGuild staff—does the talking but doesn't make decisions (bargaining committee members are in constant written communication, passing notes back and forth during sessions or talking on Slack between meetings). One side formally presents a proposal, then the other caucuses privately and returns to ask questions or present amended language. Another session is scheduled, and counter proposals offered. This back-and-forth process is slow, but decisions are made by consensus, which takes time and requires committee members to communicate with the membership.

Unions employ a range of bargaining tactics. Other shops' contracts serve as proof for convincing management to move. Says a committee member, "we're like, 'listen, this is what other contracts have, you can't lowball us, we see it in plain language in front of us. You're lying to us if you think a $32,000 base salary is industry standard.'" Committees have also presented reporters' writing on issues they want to improve through contracts to demonstrate a company's progressive commitments. A "really effective" but "sort of awful" strategy, as one worker puts it, is inviting members to share personal stories to help management understand how abstract points of contract language are real people's lived experiences. Members came to share "stories of survival" such as trying to afford rent in New York, or just trying to afford lunch. Management has to listen for sometimes up to an hour, says a union organizer, "as people describe their experiences of racial injustice in the workplace, sexual harassment in the workplace, what it's like not to get a raise, what it's like to be a single mom."

Tactics escalate when management pushes back, which they have done on several issues. Some companies have shown "stiff resistance" to intellectual property clauses, such as royalties on works produced by employees. Others were reluctant to agree to diversity and equity proposals that, for example, would require a company to interview two "diverse" candidates for every open position. "They said it was too much work," says a bargaining committee member, that "those talent pools don't exist." Says a WGAE organizer, "There is a lot of pushback from management [on diversity initiatives] particularly because contracts are enforceable, arbitrable documents. So, we get a lot of, 'look, we want to do this but we're not putting it in the contract.'" During Vice Canada negotiations, for example, the committee presented a proposal with language on sexual assault, health and safety, and racial discrimination. When management countered, "they stripped [the proposal] of all our language," says a bargaining committee member. "They took out all of the health and safety language. They took out all of the sexual harassment language . . . they didn't want to codify it, because they thought it was enough for it to be in the [employee] handbook." Workers are often surprised when management resists initiatives that don't cost money. "Pushing back against trying to improve diversity in the company, that's insane," says another member. "That was one of the more distressing parts [of bargaining]."

For others, economic issues were a challenge. A year into negotiations with Thrillist, Group Nine Media management presented a final salary floor of $40,500 per year with a 1 percent annual increase and a 1.5 percent merit-based increase. Members insisted on the inadequacy of such a salary in New York, and they met one evening to strategize about how to move management. They felt the membership was united and could be rallied around this issue, so they planned a walkout, the first in digital media. "Everyone was pretty on board," says a committee member. "Especially when we told them how adamant the company was about saying there was no money when we could see the money being spent around us." A few days later, instead of going to work, union members met at the WGAE office where they held a strike vote—again, the first digital media shop to do so. Ninety-one percent of unit members voted for a strike mandate, which meant the committee could call a strike if they believed it necessary to pressure management. The union also tweeted and posted flyers around the office with information about merit pay and making ends meet. The tactics worked; the contract stipulates a minimum salary of $50,000 and guaranteed raises.

Several other shops authorized strike votes to show solidarity and pressure management during bargaining, including Law360 (after two years at the table with no contract) and Slate. Slate union members were outraged by management's insistence that Slate be an "open shop," which means workers can choose whether or not to pay union dues. Workers wanted a closed shop, a vital form of union security, and voted 98 percent to strike if necessary. (According to an organizer, unionized workers at Foreign Policy, also owned by Graham Holdings, where union membership is optional, reached out to Slate workers to urge them to hold out for union security.) A month later, the union ratified its first contract, which includes union security. Vox union members undertook the most high-profile walkout to date, as

300 members held a one-day walkout after a year of negotiating and no agreement on wages, raises, severance, or subcontracted work (the unit had staged a one-hour walkout a month prior). Over 30 hours later, after bargaining into the night and the next morning, the committee announced that it had reached an agreement with $56,000 minimum salaries, guaranteed annual and retroactive raises, and other strong provisions.

These actions show that "winning a first contract requires much more than simply good bargaining skills," as Juravich, Bronfenbrenner, and Hickey write.[7] Key to digital media unions winning strong contracts has been keeping up the solidarity and mobilization developed during organizing drives. A strong, united membership is vital to successfully mount pressure tactics such as walkouts and strike votes, and units maintain mobilization and communication committees during the bargaining process, tasked with circulating social media content about bargaining, organizing button days (when members wear union buttons to work and post selfies on Twitter), hanging posters in their newsroom, writing collective letters to management, or orchestrating open letters from celebrities (the WGAE got 78 HBO writers to sign a statement urging Vice to reach an agreement, for example). The payoff has been strong contracts.

Digital journalism's emerging labor code

The length of journalists' contracts, from scarcely seven pages to pushing 60, is a rough indicator that these agreements vary greatly in detail and scope. Each contract is shop-specific, yet patterns emerge. The contracts are tailored to digital media work, but principal gains keep within universal union priority areas: compensation, equity, and control—labor basics that have unique bearing in the context of journalism.

Refusing to feel lucky to work in media whatever the pay, journalists organized to win higher wages. They achieved this goal in their first contracts, which return to workers a bigger slice of the value they produce and, in the process, make media livelihoods more sustainable. Salary minimums—many first contracts started at $50,000, for example—are an agreement staple. In some shops, the most underpaid employees received a whopping 20–25 percent raise. At the *Los Angeles Times*, the tentative agreement signed in October 2019 stipulates a 12.5 percent increase for all members, "with an average raise of more than $11,000."[8] According to the union, about 200 workers will receive raises of at least $10,000 once the contract is ratified, signaling strength in bargaining but also a history of low and under-payment at the paper. A pay bump of this magnitude "makes an immediate material difference in someone's life," says a WGAE organizer. Yet the implications exceed any single journalist's ability to get by in a costly media city. Fifty thousand dollars, says one journalist, is "a salary you can live on" and expands access to media careers: "the lowest-level people . . . are going to be able to pay rent, so you don't have to be a rich kid to get a job."

CBAs end the practice of individualized compensation. Agreements introduce pay scales, with salary floors organized by job title. At HuffPost, for instance, the Reporter minimum is $58,000, while the Senior Editor minimum is $70,000.[9] Like most union contracts, individuals can negotiate above minimums. Salary grids may appear to be a cold calculation, but these charts make good on journalists' frustration with previously arbitrary pay ranges. As one journalist explains, a salary chart is a "blunt instrument" to iron out disparities that result from the absence of a "compensation philosophy: it's just when you were hired, what you negotiated, whether you've been bold enough to ask for a raise." Journalists have won guaranteed, across-the-board annual raises, too, frequently in the 2–4 percent range. Prior to their first contract, says one media worker, "you'd just go on with your starting salary indefinitely, no matter what happened in the wider world."

Journalists' livelihood gains go beyond salary. Some protect members' right to do freelance work, for example. Many contain language on derivative works, or works journalists create at a publication that are turned (by the journalist or the employer) into a larger work, like a book or a film script. Slate writers, for instance, won "the right to take 100 percent royalties of any book deal."[10] Agreements codify the employer's good faith involvement of employees in reuse discussions and formalize revenue-sharing pools when the employer sells member-created content to a third-party. Gaining a 401(k), or matching retirement savings plan, realizes one of the Fast Company Union's top bargaining priorities. Other benefits directly affect members' pocketbooks and welfare, with contracts variously locking in status quo benefits or introducing new benefits; namely, medical insurance. Contracts also sustain media labor by guaranteeing time away from work, with vacation standards correcting previous disparities between staff. From pay to pension to parental leave, journalists' gains in the livelihood sphere begin to make it easier to imagine a long-term career in media.

Journalists organized to reduce the precarity of media work. Virtually all of the contracts contain a pillar of job security, "just cause," which identifies legitimate grounds for dismissal. This safeguards against scenarios ranging from a temperamental manager to vindictive firing for union activity. Just cause fosters a basic sense of safety in "knowing that you can't just be fired because your boss doesn't like you that day," says a NewsGuild organizer. But job loss fears also exist on an industrial scale. With one-quarter of US newsroom jobs shed between 2008 and 2018,[11] a looming question for workers is: how long will this publication, let alone my job within it, survive? As brands shutter, merge, and sell in a flash, "there's a much deeper sense now that the collective bargaining agreement is not going to last more than a few years," says a NewsGuild organizer. To adapt, unions have pushed for "successorship" language in their contracts that requires a new owner to inherit the agreement. The Law360 contract, for example, stipulates that the CBA "will be binding upon such successor or assignee with the same effect as if it had been originally signed by the successor or assignee."[12]

While journalists are keenly aware of their industry's volatility, contracts register their refusal to shoulder the burden of risk without basic assurances. Layoffs are "inevitable," says a journalist, but a contract "build(s) a safety net . . . so that when that stuff happens, it's a little less drastic." Ruling out the dramatic clear-your-desk situation, it's common for contracts to establish a layoff process, beginning with advance notice. The Guardian US contract stipulates 60-day notice for layoffs of a third or more of the workforce.[13] The notice period can also serve as a window for "effects bargaining." The Slate contract, for instance, allows the union to meet with the employer to discuss the cuts, including "possible alternatives to the layoffs."[14] Contracts variously outline seniority's role in layoffs, guarantee a job offer if a member's position reopens, and specify severance, which was frequently a top issue in bargaining. Severance amounts range from Law360's four weeks of pay per year of service, or two weeks of pay per year of service, whichever is greater, "up to a maximum of 26 weeks' pay"[15] to Vox's minimum of 11-weeks for up to three years of service.[16] These provisions give journalists a modicum of predictability in uncertain circumstances, enabling union staff to assure members, "Okay, this vertical just folded. Here is your union contract; here is what's going to happen in the event of layoffs; here are your rights; here is your guaranteed severance; if we get sold, here is what happens."

Contracts introduce distinct measures to address media workers' precarity, such as independent contractors, who are not directly covered by the collective agreement because they lack employee status. In some drives, a galvanizing issue was "permalancing," or media companies' practice of discounting their labor overhead by hiring workers on so many back-to-back, short-term contracts that these workers are de facto permanent employees, minus job security and benefits. To support such workers, journalists often secure a CBA provision that entitles contractors to convert to full-time status following, say, the equivalent of one year of consecutive work. Other stipulations to curb precarity include barring the employer from outsourcing unit work at the cost of layoffs (at the Guardian US), extending health benefits to part-timers (at Jacobin), and guaranteeing that interns are paid a minimum wage (at Vice Canada). Such solidaristic contract provisions are an act of collective protection within and against the wider precarious media labor economy, with many unionized journalists not only having firsthand experience as interns and freelancers, but also recognizing that they may one day rejoin the freelance pool.

Journalists organized to make their newsrooms more equitable and diverse, and their push to enhance equity is intersectional. Livelihood gains, for example, are not exclusively economic—they directly confront sexism and racism. Establishing salary minimums by title and across-the-board raises close the gendered and racialized wage gap between journalists doing equal work. Journalists have also used bargaining to challenge the white- and male-dominated constitution of newsrooms. Many drives aspired to diversify newsrooms and, as a journalist says, "you can't talk about diversity without talking about hiring." But, admits an organizer, the significant constraint is that an "employer is going to be resistant to the idea that the members have explicit approval or control over a hire." Nonetheless, new media union contracts have achieved meaningful reforms to the processes that shape newsroom composition.

A common tactic is to set recruitment criteria. Some contracts mandate that vacancies be posted publicly. This requirement is a response to what one NewsGuild organizer describes as "a deep, industry-wide problem": the hiring "pipeline," with new entrants coming up through senior managers' and editors' social circles, networks that reflect and reinforce "the privilege within the business . . . and thrive at the exclusion of people of color." Several contracts codify the employer's commitment to "endeavour to interview candidates from groups traditionally underrepresented in journalism," as written in Slate's contract.[17] Countering a management-side claim forwarded in some negotiations that candidates from marginalized groups don't apply for positions, some contracts identify specific professional networks for reaching young journalists of color, such as the National Association of Black Journalists.

The strongest contractual language on equity in recruitment follows the spirit of the National Football League's "Rooney Rule," specifying the number of candidates from under-represented groups that must be selected for interview. Intercept, for example, must interview a minimum of two members of "groups traditionally underrepresented in journalism (i.e., women, people of color, or those identifying as a LGBTQ+) prior to making a hiring decision."[18] And at Vox, half of the applicants for the "most senior positions" that "make it beyond the phone interview . . . will be from underrepresented backgrounds."[19] These requirements hold potential to widen both access to media careers and the range of media voices, with the link between newsroom composition and media representation hinted at in the Vice Media US contract, which states the union and employer's shared "commitment to diversity, equity, and inclusion in both editorial staff and coverage."[20]

Journalists organized to protect editorial independence and professional autonomy. Their contracts contain language that upholds the divide between business and editorial. Enshrined in the Gawker agreement, for example, was the position that "[d]ecisions about editorial content (e.g., whether to post a story or the story's contents, headline or placement) may only be made by editorial."[21] Some contracts also outline the procedure to be followed—including the journalist's role—when an advertiser requests that published content be removed or amended. Among the strongest defenses of journalists' autonomy are contract provisions empowering members to refuse to work on a particular project. In the Guardian US contract, journalists' control over their work is framed in terms of "integrity," stipulating "(a)n employee shall not be required to perform, over the employee's protest, any practice which in the employee's judgement compromises the employee's integrity."[22] Similarly, the Law360 contract forcefully declares:

> The Company, believing that a free press best gathers news without external pressures, and the Guild, believing that news employees should be responsible in their work only to their consciences and to their employers, agree that protection of news employees' integrity is of prime importance to their work.[23]

Invocations of journalistic autonomy take specific form in relation to sponsored content, or media content that has been paid for by an advertiser and has a promotional intent while appearing as editorial content. Agreements commonly enshrine members' right to decline to work on such content. "If a bargaining unit employee feels that such an assignment is inappropriate under the circumstances," states the Thrillist contract, "that bargaining unit employee may decline the assignment."[24] The language in the Vice US agreement is definitive: "It is understood that it is not a core job function of editorial employees to participate in the creation of sales pitches to advertisers."[25]

Finally, journalists organized to transform their workplace culture. Unions have used the collective agreement as "a mechanism to promote and sustain healthy work environments," says a NewsGuild organizer. To de-normalize excessive hours, for example, a number of contracts introduce "compensatory time," which entitles journalists to time off when they exceed standard hours, thereby reducing their unpaid labor time. Contracts also try to shift the culture of the newsroom by enhancing communication. "Key to a lot of it," says Reilly-Collins, "is transparency." Contracts require management to disclose information to the union, including member salary and demographic data, so that the union can monitor employers' progress on equity. Contracts also tackle workplace informality, which was said to have reached the level of "chaos" in one shop. Telling are the modest provisions that some journalists regard as gains, like securing access to job descriptions, regular staff meetings, and performance evaluations. While a contract is unable to summon what one journalist referred to as "a functioning HR department," unions have managed to formalize processes and introduce expectations into sometimes highly dysfunctional offices.

Equity, inclusion, and safety are core aspects of improving workplace culture. Recruitment criteria are necessary to make newsrooms "look like America," as one journalist puts it, yet, explains a NewsGuild organizer, "if the workplace culture is extremely unsupportive and toxic, [journalists of color] are going to come in and leave." Minimally, contracts enshrine protections against discrimination on the basis of race, gender, disability, immigration status, and other dimensions of oppression,[26] and some contracts affirm members' right to use their preferred pronoun. Allegations of harassment in digital media[27] give context to contracts that express employees' right to a "safe and respectful work environment."[28] By addressing "online harassment," whether it's abusive comments, trolling, or hate speech,[29] some agreements recognize that journalists' work environment extends to the social media platforms through which their work circulates. Contractual language that registers the employer's responsibility to support employees who experience harassment is not a panacea, but it does provide a tool for media workers to hold their employers to account.

Bargaining, as one media worker learned, is an opportunity not only to "negotiate conditions of employment," but also to "legislate structures into your workplace." Grievance and arbitration processes for enforcing the collective agreement as well as Weingarten Rights, or the ability of workers to have union representation in disciplinary meetings, are examples of such structures. But journalists also want access to decision-makers beyond the bargaining table. To enable this, contracts mandate the formation of various labor-management committees, which change the culture of the workplace by amplifying journalists' collective voice. Salon's labor-management committee, for example, is tasked with addressing "employee concerns . . . including, among others, diversity, training, new technology, editorial independence."[30] Some contracts establish committees devoted specifically to editorial standards and diversity and equity. While committee efficacy is limited in some contracts to information exchange and dialogue, other agreements use action-oriented language: "Wherever possible," states Law360's contract, "agreed-upon solutions will be implemented."[31] A journalist from another outlet says the labor-management committee "will be the first really formal channel for rank-and-file level input into management." As a means for members to continue to engage and pressure their employer after their contract has been signed, committee infrastructure serves to deepen unions' "institutional presence . . . in the workplace."[32]

Journalists' first contracts are documents of conviction and dignity, but also of compromise. Collective bargaining occurs within structural constraints that are most overtly expressed in a contract section usually titled "management rights." These rights, vast in scope, are a reminder of capital's power over production. Slate management, for example, asserts the right to "exercise sole discretion on all decisions involving the scope and direction of the business and all content or editorial matters," including the right—of major significance to journalistic labor—"to introduce new technology."[33]

In collective bargaining, "you kind of give a little here, and get a little there," says one media worker. In virtually all of the contracts, for example, journalists forfeited a fundamental source of workers' counterpower, the capacity to withhold their labor, by agreeing not to strike during the term of the agreement. At a different scale, the requirement to get a manager's approval on a freelance gig will annoy the journalist who could say, "'Oh, I always just got to do what I wanted,'" says an organizer. Overall, however, digital media contracts restrain capital's power and expand labor's rights. Journalists' success in clawing back managerial power over labor is perhaps most strikingly illustrated in those contracts that nullify the "non-compete" agreements through which employers have tried to restrict workers' mobility by barring them from working for a perceived competitor for a set period after they leave their jobs—this issue "galvanized" the Law360 drive.[34] As a WGAE organizer says, "negotiations are a negotiation." But, at the end of the bargaining process, "we look at what we won overall."

What's in a gain?

In their first contracts, digital journalists have made significant gains in the areas of livelihood, precarity, diversity and equity, editorial integrity, and workplace culture. The conclusion that Juravich, Bronfenbrenner, and Hickey reach in their multi-sector study of first contracts holds for the new media unions: "While some unions are more successful in some areas than others, clearly these contracts provide the foundation for a fundamentally different employment relationship than that which existed prior to the union organizing campaign."[35] Journalists' capacity to transform their working conditions through first contracts derives from conjunctural factors, negotiating acumen, and—decisively—media workers' power.

Yet first contracts are just a starting point. For one, a contract is only as strong as members' willingness to enforce it. As a journalist-organizer at one shop told us before their bargaining had concluded, "we have to lean on the company really hard after this contract is negotiated." A first contract is also a starting point because newly unionized media workers will face the challenge of preserving and building upon gains in the next rounds of negotiations, and enforcing a contract with management, who also have to adjust to the new reality of working under a collective agreement.

Looking beyond an individual shop, first contracts are a resource within the digital media union movement more widely. Contract language in one shop can be picked up at another to argue that proposals are reasonable and consistent with the industry's emerging labor standards. And crucially, first contracts are a communicative device that fuels the circulation of struggles. As one journalist remarks, "you watch places go through [layoffs] with a union contract, and then watch them when they don't have it, and it's just so stark, the differences . . . I think it's probably helped propel unionization drives." First contracts generate a sense of "union efficacy"[36] within journalists' professional communities. Ultimately, says Reilly-Collins, the politically significant "gain" is not so much, say, a severance package or a guaranteed annual raise: "what I see as a gain is for people to have class consciousness and to believe that collective action works."

Notes

1 Fast Company Union (@FastCoUnion), "We have excellent news," tweet, June 7, 2019, https://twitter.com/FastCoUnion/status/1137042054977130496.
2 Tom Juravich, Kate Bronfenbrenner, and Robert Hickey, "Significant Victories: An Analysis of Union First Contracts," in *Justice on the Job: Perspectives on the Erosion of Collective Bargaining in the United States*, eds. Richard N. Block, Sheldon Friedman, Michelle Kaminski, and Andy Levin (Kalamazoo: W.E. Upjohn Institute for Employment Research, 2006), 87.
3 Karl E. Klare, "Labor Law as Ideology: Toward a New Historiography of Collective Bargaining Law," *Industrial Relations Law Journal* 4, no. 3 (1981): 452, 453.
4 Colleen Shalby (@CShalby), "It's been 14 months since @latguild's bargaining committee started contract negotiations," tweet, September 3, 2019, https://twitter.com/CShalby/status/1168950614023385088.
5 Hans Rollman, "Should Unions Say No to Closed-Door Negotiations?," *Briarpatch*, June 28, 2018, https://briarpatchmagazine.com/articles/view/should-unions-say-no-to-closed-door-negotiations.
6 Andrew McCormick, "A Law Firm in the Trenches against Media Unions," *Columbia Journalism Review*, December 13, 2018, www.cjr.org/analysis/jones-day-unions-slate-strike.php.
7 Juravich, Bronfenbrenner, and Hickey, "Significant Victories," 109.
8 L.A. Times Guild, "Contract Summary and Highlights," 2019, https://static1.squarespace.com/static/59f32b4b12abd94fac1a508b/t/5da7c1c24e131701f4efb48b/1571275203091/Contract+Summary+%281%29.pdf.

9 *Agreement between the Huffington Post and the Writers Guild of America, East*, Article 15, Compensation.

10 *Agreement between Slate Magazine and the Writers Guild of America, East*, Article VIII, Derivative Work, p. 15.

11 Elizabeth Grieco, "U.S. Newsroom Employment Has Dropped by a Quarter since 2008, with Greatest Decline at Newspapers," *Pew Research Center*, July 9, 2019, www.pewresearch.org/fact-tank/2019/07/09/u-s-newsroom-employment-has-dropped-by-a-quarter-since-2008/.

12 *Collective Bargaining Agreement between Portfolio Media, Inc. d/b/a Law360 & the NewsGuild of New York, Local 31003, CWA*, December 19, 2018–December 31, 2022, Article—Successorship, 42.

13 *News Media Guild: Guardian US Collective Bargaining Agreement*, 2017–2020, Article 6—Security, 6.

14 *Agreement between Slate Magazine and the Writers Guild of America, East*, Article VI, Discipline, Discharge and Reduction in Force, 3.b, 11.

15 *Collective Bargaining Agreement between Portfolio Media, Inc. d/b/a Law360 & the NewsGuild of New York, Local 31003, CWA*, December 19, 2018–December 31, 2022, Article—Severance, Section 2, 40.

16 Writers Guild of America, East, "Vox Media Ratifies Landmark First Contract with Writers Guild of America, East," *WGAE, Press Room*, June 14, 2019, www.wgaeast.org/vox-media-ratifies-landmark-first-contract-with-writers-guild-of-america-east/.

17 *Agreement between Slate Magazine and the Writers Guild of America, East*, Article IX, Job Openings, 3, 17.

18 *Collective Bargaining Agreement between the Writers Guild of America, East and First Look Media Works, Inc.*, Article 7—Diversity, d. Open Job Positions, i., 5.

19 Writers Guild of America, East, "Vox Media Ratifies Landmark First Contract."

20 *Collective Bargaining Agreement, Writers Guild of America, East and Vice Media, LLC*, January 1, 2019–December 31, 2021, Article 19—Representation, Diversity, Equity, Inclusion, 16.

21 *Collective Bargaining Agreement, Writers Guild of America, East and Gawker Media*, Article VIII—Editorial Independence, 4.

22 *News Media Guild: Guardian US Collective Bargaining Agreement*, 2017–2020, Article 25—Employee Integrity.

23 *Collective Bargaining Agreement between Portfolio Media, Inc. d/b/a Law360 & the NewsGuild of New York, Local 31003, CWA*, December 19, 2018–December 31, 2022, Article—Indemnification and Confidentiality, 38.

24 *Collective Bargaining Agreement, Writers Guild of America, East and Thrillist Media Group, Inc.*, 2018–2021, 10.

25 *Collective Bargaining Agreement, Writers Guild of America, East and Vice Media, LLC*, January 1, 2019–December 31, 2021, Article 24—Editorial Independence, 18.

26 See, for example, *Collective Bargaining Agreement, Writers Guild of America, East and Vice Media, LLC*, Article 6—Non-Discrimination, 5.

27 Emily Steel, "At Vice, Cutting-Edge Media and Old-School Allegations of Sexual Harassment," *New York Times*, December 23, 2017, www.nytimes.com/2017/12/23/business/media/vice-sexual-harassment.html.

28 *Collective Bargaining Agreement, Writers Guild of America, East and Vice Media, LLC*, January 1, 2019–December 31, 2021, Article 17—Health & Safety/Sexual Harassment/Workplace Culture, 14.

29 *Collective Bargaining Agreement, Writers Guild of America, East and Vice Media, LLC,* January 1, 2019–December 31, 2021, Article 18—Cyber-Security and Online Harassment, 15.

30 *Collective Bargaining Agreement between Salon Media Group and the Writers Guild of America, East,* October 12, 2018–December 31, 2021, Article 5—Labor-Management Committee, 4.

31 *Collective Bargaining Agreement between Portfolio Media, Inc. d/b/a Law360 & the NewsGuild of New York, Local 31003, CWA,* December 19, 2018–December 31, 2022, Article—Joint Committee, 24.

32 Juravich, Bronfenbrenner, and Hickey, "Significant Victories," 111.

33 *Agreement between Slate Magazine and the Writers Guild of America, East,* Article IV, Management and Editorial Rights, 7.

34 The NewsGuild of New York, Local 310003, CWA, "Law360 Union Members Secure Progressive, Strong First Contract," December 18, 2018, www.nyguild.org/post/law360-union-members-secure-progressive-strong-first-contract.

35 Juravich, Bronfenbrenner, and Hickey, "Significant Victories," 111.

36 See Rebecca Kolins Givan and Lena Hipp, "Public Perceptions of Union Efficacy: A Twenty-Four Country Study," *Labor Studies Journal* 37, no. 1 (2012): 7–32.

6 Transformation

180

The Vox Media union drive was in full swing in November 2017 when Vox journalist German Lopez took to Twitter to play the killjoy. He tweeted standard anti-union lines—unions protect "lazy" workers, for example—and declared that unions may be beneficial to "lower-skilled workers" but are unnecessary for media professionals, who are treated decently by their employer and enjoy career mobility.[1] Leap ahead to August 2019, and Lopez made a highly public *mea culpa*. His platform was Vox itself, where a collective bargaining agreement was freshly in place. "I was skeptical of unions. Then I joined one," reads the headline of Lopez's lengthy article. In it, he refers to his earlier social media posts as his "worst tweets of all time" and admits doing "a complete 180 on unions." Lopez had even joined Vox Media Union's bargaining committee. He credits his about-face to "good organizing," to realizing his job was not uniquely immune from industry tumult, and to a core journalistic competency: research. Weighing a heap of evidence, Lopez concludes that unions, on balance, reduce income inequality and advance progressive social policy to the benefit of union and non-union workers alike. His article, which pro-union journalist peers shared widely, ends on a wish: "I hope more Americans go through the transformation that I did. We'd all be better for it."

Journalists' belief that they could transform their conditions for the better by unionizing continues to fuel a surge of labor organizing in which over 60 media outlets have unionized since 2015. Guided by the insights of the journalist-organizers and union staff we interviewed, this book tells a story of the collective action sweeping the digital media industry. In the previous chapters, we traced the organizing process to demystify unionization for unorganized media workers, but also to position labor as an active agent with a stake in and a vision for journalism's future. Our account began by identifying journalists' motivations to organize, including improving pay and benefits, employment security, newsroom diversity, editorial integrity, and workplace communication. We then outlined contextual factors that helped activate union drives, such as journalists' access to the legal right to collective representation, parent unions' commitment to organizing new members, and a social climate of resurgent feminist, anti-racist, and class politics and critique. Next, we documented how journalists mobilized support to unionize their workplace, from engaging coworkers in one-on-one conversations to informing management about their desire to unionize and taking their drives public. We detailed journalists' struggles to get their employers to officially recognize their union, showing that while many unions were recognized promptly, several drives confronted aggressive anti-unionism from management. We considered the negotiations phase, during which journalists' efforts to secure a first contract frequently involved using social media to pressure brand-sensitive employers to meet unions' demands. And we concluded with a review of collective bargaining agreements, finding that contractual gains varied by shop but generally lived up to journalists' initial aspirations to organize.

It's too early to fully assess the implications of the new media unions (when we conducted interviews, some unions had only recently signed their first agreements and bargaining was ongoing at some outlets). Nonetheless, we have glimpsed how journalists, newsrooms, and unions have been transformed by organizing, and it's on these inklings of transformation that we conclude.

Workers first

A journalist whose pay was set to jump by a quarter when minimum salaries took effect expressed their gratitude to a bargaining team member, saying, "My quality of life is about to go up dramatically." This journalist, says the bargaining team member, "was living in a really tough place," and with this raise "she was going to be able to move. . . . We did have to put in a lot of work, but it was not for nothing. These are really significant changes." Indeed, unionization's material impact is most immediately felt by individual journalists. From the permalancer whose position transitions to full-time, to the laid-off journalist whose severance package keeps them afloat between jobs, new media unions have won bread-and-butter contractual gains that are transforming journalists' livelihoods, especially for media workers who, prior to organizing, were the lowest paid and the least secure; often women and racialized workers.

Beyond returning to journalists a greater share of the economic value their labor produces, unionization has been personally, politically, and professionally transformative for journalists involved in campaigns and bargaining. Several campaign leaders mention organizing's intrinsic rewards and describe their participation in a union drive as a professional high point—several even contemplated a new career in the labor movement. Bearing witness to collective action's transformative impact has left lasting impressions on journalist-organizers, whether it's dispelling the lingering assumption that unions are "just for, you know, auto workers" to stoking a "feeling of possibility" among media workers. "This is the first time that, for a lot of us, it's felt like we had some control over our own destiny," says a journalist.

For some journalists, the organizing process counteracted their work's emotional burdens. Organizing, says a writer,

> has been good for my mental health. A lot of the time, we as journalists look at the state of the world and get very depressed. One of the cures for me has been to stand up for our newsroom and for other news-rooms. It has given me renewed hope in the industry.

Such hopefulness arises from transformations within journalists' professional subjectivity, as the organizing experience challenges the individualization of media work and the tendency to view peers competitively. The culture of metrics, which pressures journalists to tailor their work to attract the most page views and clicks, "keeps people working in silos, keeps them competitive," says a journalist. Likewise, in professional networks, "you're always putting on this façade, 'Everything's great!'" admits another journalist. She contrasts this performative optimism to the political sociality of new media union gatherings, where, she says, she's been able to access "the most sincere professional network I have in New York." Another journalist echoes this sentiment: "when you get us in a room, we all have the same things we care about. Even if [we] are competitors, that doesn't matter, because this [movement] is bigger than that."

Writing about digital media organizing in *The New Republic*, journalist Clio Chang observes, "media workers are increasingly seeing themselves as workers first"—a significant shift in journalistic subjectivity.[2] As one union organizer argues, "When we look at systemic oppression and the distribution of wealth in this country, most white-collar journalists have far more in common with blue-collar workers." Organizers are careful not to universalize the embrace of a worker identity among journalists, but they observe a marked generational shift. Union campaigns spurred this shift by spreading an alternative to status quo journalistic discourses of professionalism and entrepreneurialism, a "labor rights paradigm" that, says one journalist, "gives us a framework to talk honestly about our work and how it affects us." Core to this paradigm is the argument that media livelihoods will not become more sustainable with a polished personal brand, rapport with a boss, or any other individualized behavior, but instead require solidarity between media workers.

Healing it

From the recruitment process to sponsored-content assignments, a host of workplace protocols can be contractually bound to change when a newsroom's collective bargaining agreement (CBA) comes into effect. More broadly, journalist-organizers highlight shifts in two aspects of workplace culture after they unionized: communication and morale. "Prior to being organized," recalls one journalist, "we didn't have an opportunity to really participate in conversations and try to enact positive change." He says it's been "empowering to have a voice in ways I didn't anticipate." While CBAs have formalized a channel for worker voice through contractually mandated labor-management committees, journalists say that unionization also amplified worker voice in a less official and more diffuse way by fostering an atmosphere of confidence, so that people "feel more comfortable providing direct input." This reflects the potential of unions to democratize workplace relations, a process that journalist-organizer Kristina Bui tweets she witnessed firsthand at the *Los Angeles Times*: "A union will absolutely change the culture of your newsroom. @latguild empowered ours to speak out against pay inequity and discrimination, bloated executive salaries, harassment. Our newsroom culture was once based on fear and anxiety. Now we're healing it."[3]

Journalist-organizers have been looking beyond their own newsrooms since the early days of the "wave": they aspire to raise labor standards across the digital media industry. While union density in digital media remains a work in progress, union proliferation and visibility signal that a cultural shift has occurred in the digital media sector, at the center of which is the consolidation of a set of expectations and values: *sustainability*, or greater employment stability and protections against industry volatility; *accessibility*, setting salaries at levels that do not exclude all but the economically privileged; *equity*, from closing gendered and racialized wage gaps to expanding the voices of underrepresented groups in journalism; and *integrity*, which reasserts journalistic ideals of editorial independence, the necessity of just-cause provisions to safeguard journalists' ability to speak out, and protection against discrimination and harassment. New media unionism's proposition is, in part, that strengthening the employment relationship, democratizing the workplace, and revitalizing journalism are interdependent.

Newly unionized journalists acknowledge that wider organizing goals to shake up newsroom priorities won't be achieved overnight. "Baby steps" is how one journalist describes her employer's action on equity, for example. Progress toward union objectives, whether they be improving newsroom diversity or strengthening worker voice, requires members who exercise their union's counterpower and apply ongoing pressure. As one journalist-organizer notes, "Is it really a union if you have a lot of people who are reluctant to use the leverage they actually have for fear of incurring the wrath of management?" So, to ask a vital question: what kind of unions will new media unions be? To start, these unions embed within newsrooms an infrastructure of care. Journalists tell us that unions have quickly come to serve as a support resource, helping individual members understand their rights in situations ranging from taking maternity leave to being laid off. And when a conflict arises between a media worker and management, reports a Guardian US shop steward, "people feel comfortable coming to me . . . and voicing their concerns, and we are able to then approach management and get answers for people. That is not how it used to be."

Journalist-organizers are not presumptuous about their union's future. They recognize that unions can gradually retreat into a "service delivery thing," for example. A related challenge is to sustain rank-and-file participation in the institutional life of the union. Says one journalist-organizer, "After we got the contract and things got better and people got raises, people were like, 'Okay, so that's done.'" But enforcing a collective agreement, advancing union priorities, and maintaining workplace solidarity require ongoing effort, whether it's filing grievances, hosting union events, serving on labor-management committees, or mobilizing unit members to push back against management when conflict emerges. A union's capacity on these fronts is shaped by the organizing process,[4] including a drive's pace. "People tend to herald the speed at which digital media outlets have organized," one union staffer tells us. He cautions against celebrating this characteristic, arguing that rapidly formed labor organizations are "necessarily weaker," because they are more likely to lack the camaraderie and education among union members that prepares them to effectively counter management in the long run. Similarly, a journalist warns against the "we-just-want-to-win-a-contract" mindset, emphasizing that the ultra-fast campaign's cost is cutting short conversation among workers "about what the point of having a union is; what does it mean for working people to have power within their workplace?"

The overwhelming majority of the media union drives that emerged during our study succeeded. But some organizing efforts didn't get to the point to test a union's power to transform a newsroom. Management defeated union drives at Canada's *National Post* and at BuzzFeed News UK.[5] Gothamist and DNAinfo journalists successfully unionized, but owner Joe

Ricketts shuttered the entire company (even though only the New York offices unionized). Al Jazeera America ceased operations before its fledgling union negotiated a contract.[6] And, after unionizing, Mic was sold to Bustle Media Group and more than 100 staff were laid off, a move that former Mic employees saw as an attempt to "break Mic's editorial union."[7] Anti-union closures, sudden buy-outs, and blanket layoffs are stark reminders of media capital's structural power, particularly that of ownership. And yet, such announcements have validated rather than suppressed journalists' impulse to organize. On the heels of a mass layoff at Mic, for example, the defiant Mic Union published an open letter with eight recommendations for fellow media workers. Recommendation number one: "Unionize your newsroom!"[8]

Journalists' labor struggles have gained visibility through union-produced counter-publicity on social media and ample coverage by established media, including recently unionized outlets. This raises a wider question: how might the new media unions affect the coverage of labor and workers' struggles—a historically marginalized news topic—on a broad scale?[9] Journalists we interviewed are hesitant to predict a full-fledged comeback for the labor beat, but they certainly see connections between the union campaigns and media content. "I would hope that journalists, through their own unionization efforts, are more fluent in labor issues," says Amanda Holpuch, who helped organize at The Guardian US. Another journalist sees media unions having "trickle-down effect: it changes the conversation about labor [in] the media." While a number of outlets were covering labor issues before their staff unionized, one journalist's impression is that "it's much more common, I feel, to have reporting from a labor-centric perspective in these [unionized] outlets." The pro-union Vox article we mentioned at the start of this chapter supports this view. "Probably one of the biggest effects of all of these media unions," this journalist adds, "is public consciousness." It is on this point that media outlets are a strategic sector for the wider labor movement, not necessarily on account of the digital media industry's economic significance, but based on the social function of media as producers of the symbolic resources through which the social world is framed and understood.[10] By the same token, media unions' push for newsroom diversity is not simply about demographic representation in a quantified sense. Instead, it is about the relationship between newsroom composition and media content, or which stories are told and who gets to tell them.[11]

More unions everywhere

Over 60 successful media union drives in under five years is a bright spot for the embattled labor movement. In 2018, union membership in the United States slumped to 10.5 percent, the country's lowest union-density figure on record.[12] Unions' declining presence and social and political influence, particularly since the 1980s, is typically chalked up to external factors such as the globalization of production, the flexibilization of labor, the expansion of industries without union traditions, and the entrenchment of anti-worker policy and ideology under neoliberalism. But the crisis of unions is also the product of factors internal to the labor movement: "racism and sexism, retrograde valorization of toil and hostility to environmental protection, bureaucratic complacency, institutional rigidity . . . need we continue?" writes a labor activist.[13]

Digital journalists' organizing streak is a textbook case of what labor activists and scholars call "union renewal," or "processes of change to 'put new life and vigour' in the labour movement and to rebuild organisational and institutional strength."[14] Goals, commitments, and activities encompassed by the union renewal idea include organizing the unorganized, boosting rank-and-file participation, experimenting with organizing strategies, expanding the diversity of union staff and leadership, and engaging with social movements.[15] Digital media organizing contributes to the transformation of unionism by reaffirming principles and practices associated with the wider, collective project of union renewal.

New media unions support labor struggles within and beyond media. Journalists celebrate their unions' recognition and publicize contractual gains on social media, which energizes union formation. This is important because "in the absence of significant victories," writes union researcher Gregor Murray, "workers are less inclined to undertake collective action."[16] As we have seen, new media union members enact cross-shop solidarity by sharing their organizing experience with professional peers from other outlets who are embarking on campaigns. Journalists' job mobility is a medium of union diffusion, too: when a journalist-organizer leaves a position at a union shop and starts a new role at a non-union newsroom, they bring with them know-how to potentially support a fresh unionization effort.

We increasingly see how new media unions' influence overspills newsrooms. Digital journalists' collective action inspired temps at Google to protest the mistreatment of contract workers,[17] encouraged art handlers at the Guggenheim Museum in New York to launch a union drive,[18] and anticipated the campaign Game Workers Unite, which aims to organize video game developers.[19] More broadly, unionized journalists support labor causes by making media contributions to a "pro-worker political ecology."[20] Spotlighting labor issues on social media and writing about labor makes journalists feel part of a larger labor movement. Says an organizer, "the cultural influence that the individual members have is way-outsized for the number of people we're organizing." Few unions have members among their ranks with occupational access to public communication platforms where it is possible to declare, as Lopez does in his Vox article, "We need more unions everywhere."

The media worker campaign surge has prompted change within parent media unions, too. The growing number of journalists reaching out to unions to discuss organizing has pressed the unions to take seriously a twin requirement of union revitalization: to "[renew] their commitment to organizing"[21] and to allocate increased resources to it. New media unions not only continue the 20th-century tradition of organizing legacy media, but also extend union presence to digital-first publications, an instance of what activist-scholar Sam Gindin describes as the "breakthroughs in new sectors critical to union revival."[22] Organizing digital journalists prepares the labor movement to organize new constituencies in adjacent fields, such as digital cultural industries and the tech sector. "We're going to see more of these types of workers organizing that we wouldn't have even thought five years ago would be organizing," predicts a NewsGuild organizer.

Parent unions are affected by new media unions beyond membership growth. Newly unionized journalists' bargaining priorities have generated innovative contract language regarding, for example, equity in recruitment and gender pronouns, and have also elevated demands, such as succession clauses, that promise to strengthen parent unions' model contracts. New media union members have also pushed efforts to support precarious media workers. While some CBAs have extended protections to contractors, the employment-based union model has limited ability to improve freelancers' conditions. In response, digital media union activists who had experience organizing in newsrooms have developed the Freelance Solidarity Project. Launched in 2019, the project was organized by workers who had been through WGAE campaigns, and incubated for a year and a half by the WGAE, which provided office space for meetings and hosted a two-day summit. The Freelance Solidarity Project is now a membership division of the National Writers Union, and will work with multiple unions toward the goal of setting and raising industry standards for media freelancers.[23] New media unions have also produced a new generation of activist members keen on changing the very top of the union structure. At time of writing, the NewsGuild-CWA's long-serving president, Bernie Lunzer, was in a fraught election contest with a young data journalist who helped lead the union drive at the *Los Angeles Times*, Jon Schleuss, whose election platform argues that the NewsGuild must step up its game on multiple fronts, from organizing to equity, from international solidarity to union communication.[24]

Digital media unionism must navigate a corporate landscape that has become "more volatile and unpredictable" recently, one journalist-organizer tells us. Indeed, layoffs, closures, mergers, and acquisitions are happening quickly. "More than 1,000 employees lost their jobs this year in layoffs at

BuzzFeed, AOL, Yahoo, HuffPost and Vice Media," the *New York Times* reported in September 2019.[25] These layoffs are a reminder of the necessity of winning contracts with severance provisions and effects-bargaining rights. The digital media industry is not only precarious, but is marked by perpetually shifting and consolidating ownership. "In 2020, we will continue to see even more mergers and acquisitions," predicts a Bustle Media Group executive.[26] Whether these maneuvers are owners' measures to prevent an outlet from shutting down, to reach new audiences, to diversify media formats, or to reduce dependency on digital advertising, mergers and acquisitions in the digital media industry are accumulation strategies that have potentially significant consequences for new media unions. For one, they raise the significance of succession rights as a bargaining priority. And as one journalist-organizer points out, some mergers have placed bargaining units affiliated with different parent media unions under the same owner. For example, in 2019, Vox Media, a WGAE shop, acquired New York Media, which publishes *New York* magazine, a NewsGuild shop.[27] The speed of ownership changes in digital media, says a journalist-organizer, means that media workers may need to be prepared to confront a merger or acquisition midway through their mobilizing phase. As for media conglomerates, they may present unions with a strategic opportunity to coordinate organizing campaigns across brands, as suggested by the November 2019 announcement that media workers at 24 outlets in the Hearst Communications empire were ready to unionize with the WGAE. Such developments inch the digital media industry closer to the prospect of sectoral bargaining. Whatever the outcome, digital media organizing will have to coevolve with a rapidly shifting lineup of corporate players.

As for how organizing strategies have been transformed by the digital media union movement, union staffers say that new media union drives have not fundamentally departed from longstanding organizing principles. One-on-one conversations and raising workers' expectations, for example, remain essential. And yet, working with digital journalists has prompted union organizers to further hone active organizing models and heed calls for greater transparency and democratic participation. While "no single strategy is sufficient to restore union influence,"[28] digital media drives seem to share several characteristics that were consistently vital to victory. Bread-and-butter grievances, as we've seen, motivated a number of campaigns. But media workers' commitment to unionization is often tied to wider issues and aspirations—sustainability, accessibility, equity, and integrity, for example—and the call to raise labor standards across the digital media industry. This echoes researchers' claim that "for unions to be strategic, they should pursue [a] vocabulary of motive that seeks a larger purpose."[29]

Similarly, the themes that now regularly appear in journalists' why-we-are-organizing communiques support the view that "[t]he ability to provide overarching narratives as a frame of reference for union action is . . . a key factor in union renewal."[30]

The unionization drives in our study solidify commitment to rank-and-file engagement. Specifically, historically excluded workers, including women and people of color, are taking leadership roles in this transformation by initiating drives, leading or serving on organizing committees, and participating in bargaining and post-contract committees. The digital media union movement underscores the strategic importance of workers' autonomy in organizing. While union campaigns are rooted in relationships of trust, education, and guidance between staff organizers and inside organizers, the drives tend to have a strong self-organization aspect to them, which pre-empts several angles of anti-union rhetoric. Welcoming and encouraging journalists' participation in the campaign has enabled organizers to recognize and leverage media workers' communicative resources and online habitat. Organizing in digital media has been especially inventive in the sphere of tactics, including harnessing social media to make struggles visible beyond the workplace, using digital tools like electronic authorization cards and Google documents to organize, holding creative workplace actions to express newsroom solidarity, testing new forms of digital workplace disruption such as the "Slack strike," and practicing "open" bargaining. Such tactics, and their strategic escalation, have been decisive to organizing victories and securing strong contracts. Broadening the base of engagement, such tactics contribute to the factor that ultimately decides the outcome of a labor struggle: workers' bargaining power.

Cultures of solidarity

Cultures of solidarity, as Fantasia writes, "can shape class relations in significant ways."[31] To achieve this in the media industry, digital journalists are waging a struggle to transform expectations in their sector. Says one journalist-organizer, "a lot of the stuff that [journalists have] internalized as totally standard workplace practice is actually really fucked up . . . We've learned to accept a lot of stuff that is not actually acceptable." Echoing Jane McAlevey's claim that organizing is fundamentally about "raising expectations,"[32] another journalist hopes that the "organizing drives across shops is a way of building expectations for writers. . . . Just because something's been this way up until now, doesn't mean it has to stay that way." Raising journalists' expectations—and demonstrating that, under specific conditions, employers can be pressured to better meet those expectations—is a central thread in the digital media unionism story that also carries wider political relevance. As Gindin says:

> Working people generally know that things suck. The problem is that they don't believe that things can change. . . . Organization helps overcome that by making gains, or even lessons from defeats, add up to something. More generally, people need organizations that can give them some hope and confidence that working and struggling through them matters.[33]

One of the most central features of digital media unionism is that expressions of mutuality exceed the bounds of a single newsroom. Cultures of solidarity, writes Fantasia, help foster "values of mutual solidarity," including "a new sense of 'us,' a new sense of 'them,' and emergent moral sensibilities about the values associated with each."[34] This is captured by a journalist-organizer when she describes the need to distinguish journalists' relations to each other from the market relations within and between outlets:

> Publications are all set up to be in competition with each other. We are often publishing similar things and fighting for clicks. But the whole union organizing process [has shown] we're all part of the same workforce that is being pretty systematically screwed. . . . People are not having an easy time in media.

Referring to how journalist-organizers support emergent drives, she adds, "Knowing that we can be an inspiration to other places that are not unionized yet, and showing what we could get and what changes are possible—that's a really big thing."

Beyond raising journalists' expectations, the digital media union movement has heightened journalists' willingness to escalate labor action. Take, for instance, the events that rattled the sports, culture, and politics site Deadspin, a WGAE shop, in October 2019.[35] Part of G/O Media, Deadspin is owned by private equity firm Great Hill Partners. Deadspin writers' discontent with management had already been simmering when a top editor received a directive to only publish sports content. Refusing to enforce the injunction, the editor was fired. Deadspin writers continued to flaunt the directive, believing that they understood better than their new owner the content that performed well for the business.[36] Then, after meeting about the firing of their editor, staff started to resign en masse: within about a week, all 20 Deadspin journalists had quit, announcing their resignations on Twitter. Collectively taking the exit option, Deadspin writers offered a reminder that workers' power resides in their capacity to withdraw labor. The resignations, which made headlines, reveals the limits of journalists' willingness to acquiesce to management and the livelihood risks that some journalists are willing to take. The Deadspin episode returns us to cultures of solidarity, which, as Fantasia suggests, are not rooted in innate fellow feeling. Rather, "cultures of solidarity . . . are formed out of friction": employers' actions serve "as the *source* of solidarity."[37] It's difficult to imagine the Deadspin resignations happening in the absence of the politicization of journalist subjectivity linked to the digital media union movement over nearly five years. Unionization in digital media "created an opening for workers to rethink what they are settling for and how to take matters in their own hands," writes journalist Alexia Fernández Campbell. "In a way," Fernández Campbell adds,

> the Deadspin resignations bring the (digital media) labor movement full circle. After all, it was Deadspin's sister site, Gawker, that set off the movement to unionize in digital media. Now writers are demanding more than better pay and benefits. They want more control over their work. In quitting, Deadspin employees took control.[38]

In the context of struggles against deepening class inequality, digital media unions are not alone. There has been an upsurge of militant labor organizing among teachers and low-wage service workers in the United States; robust campaigns to increase the minimum wage across Canada and the United States; bids to unionize and organize gig workers; and a turn to labor politics by white-collar and millennial workers, including adjunct professors, grad students, tech workers, and art and cultural workers. Our study demonstrates that digital media is not just a strategic site for capital investment and profit seeking, and not just a site of employment for journalists today, but also a strategic site for the labor movement. Digital media are vital for renewing union organizing, and can have implications for the broader labor movement in terms of building solidarity, generating more nuanced coverage of labor struggles, and promoting union membership at a time when organized labor is under attack.

Notes

1 German Lopez, "I Was Skeptical of Unions: Then I Joined One," *Vox*, August 19, 2019, www.vox.com/policy-and-politics/2019/8/19/20727283/unions-good-income-inequality-wealth.
2 Clio Chang, "How to Save Journalism," *The New Republic*, July 11, 2019, https://newrepublic.com/article/154455/save-journalism.

3 Kristina Bui (@kbui1), "A union will absolutely change the culture of your newsroom," tweet, March 18, 2019, https://twitter.com/kbui1/status/11076848 30022500359?s=11.

4 Linda Markowitz, "After the Organizing Ends: Workers, Self-Efficacy, Activism, and Union Frameworks," *Social Problems* 45, no. 3 (1998): 356–82.

5 H.G. Watson, "No Union at National Post after CWA Canada Loses Certification Vote," *J-Source*, April 27, 2018, https://j-source.ca/article/no-union-at-national-post-after-cwa-canada-loses-certification-vote/; Jim Waterson, "BuzzFeed UK Staff Reject Chance to Unionize," *The Guardian*, July 18, 2018, www.theguardian.com/media/2018/jul/18/buzzfeed-uk-staff-reject-chance-to-join-nuj.

6 E. Tammy Kim, "Unionizing the Digital Newsroom," *Dissent*, July 19, 2016, www.dissentmagazine.org/online_articles/unionizing-digital-newsroom.

7 Benjamin Goggin, "Did Mic Layoff Their Entire Editorial Staff Ahead of Their Sale to Bustle Media Group to Break a Union?," *Business Insider*, December 1, 2018, www.businessinsider.com/mic-layoff-bustle-union-labor.

8 Mic Union, "From Mic Union to Media Management: We Are Watching," *The NewsGuild of New York*, January 18, 2019, www.nyguild.org/front-page-details/from-mic-union-resolutions-for-digital-media.

9 William Puette, *Through Jaundiced Eyes: How the Media View Organized Labour* (Ithaca: Cornell University Press, 1992); Christopher R. Martin, *Framed! Labor and the Corporate Media* (Ithaca: Cornell University Press, 2004).

10 David Hesmondhalgh, *The Cultural Industries*, 3rd Edition (London: Sage, 2013), 4.

11 See Anamik Saha, *Race and the Cultural Industries* (Cambridge: Polity Press, 2018).

12 Doug Henwood, "Unions Still Haven't Rebounded," *Jacobin*, January 25, 2019, www.jacobinmag.com/2019/01/union-density-united-states-2018-bls.

13 Gabriel Winant, "Who Works for the Workers?," *N+1*, 26 (Fall 2016), https://nplusonemag.com/issue-26/essays/who-works-for-the-workers/.

14 Gregor Murray, "Union Renewal: What Can We Learn from Three Decades of Research?," *Transfer* 23, no. 1 (2017): 10.

15 See: Pradeep Kumar and Christopher Schenk, "Union Renewal and Organizational Change: A Review of the Literature," in *Paths to Union Renewal: The Canadian Experience*, eds. Pradeep Kumar and Christopher Schenk (Guelph: Broadview Press, 2006), 29–60; Charlotte Yates, "The Road to Union Renewal: From Organizing the Unorganized to New Political Alternatives," *Canadian Dimension*, March 1, 2004, https://canadiandimension.com/articles/view/the-road-to-union-renewal-from-organizing-the-unorganized-to-new-political-.

16 Murray, "Union Renewal," 15.

17 Julia Carrie Wong, "Google Staff Condemn Treatment of Temp Workers in 'Historic' Show of Solidarity," *The Guardian*, April 2, 2019, www.theguardian.com/technology/2019/apr/02/google-workers-sign-letter-temp-contractors-protest.

18 Elizabeth A. Harris and Robin Pogrebin, "Inside Hushed Museum Hallways, a Rumble Over Low Pay Grows Louder," *New York Times*, July 22, 2019, www.nytimes.com/2019/07/22/arts/museum-pay-unions.html.

19 Aron Garst, "How Video Game Unionization Would Happen," *Variety*, December 17, 2018, https://variety.com/2018/gaming/features/video-game-industry-union-unionization-1203091114/.

20 Richard Croucher and Geoffrey Wood, "Union Renewal in Historical Perspective," *Work, Employment & Society* 31, no. 6 (2017): 1018.

21 Yates, "The Road to Union Renewal."

22 Sam Gindin, cited in Chris Maisano, "The Crisis in American Labor: An Interview with Sam Gindin," *Jacobin*, January 8, 2019, https://jacobinmag.com/2013/02/sam-gindin-on-the-crisis-in-american-labor/.

23 National Writers Union, "Freelance Solidarity Project," accessed October 15, 2019, https://nwu.org/freelance-solidarity-project/.

24 Joshua Benton, "America's Largest Union of Journalists Is Doing a Rewrite of Its Leadership Election," *NiemanLab*, August 14, 2019, www.niemanlab.org/2019/08/americas-largest-union-of-journalists-is-doing-a-rewrite-of-its-leadership-election/; see Jon Schleuss, "Jon's Platform," accessed October 15, 2019, www.jonforpresident.com/platform.

25 Marc Tracy and Edmund Lee, "Vox Media Acquires New York Magazine, Chronicler of the Highbrow and Lowbrow," *The New York Times*, September 24, 2019, www.nytimes.com/2019/09/24/business/media/vox-buys-nymag.html.

26 Sara Jerde, "Media Mergers Aren't New: So Why Are Publishers Consolidating Now?," *Adweek*, October 14, 2019, www.adweek.com/digital/media-mergers-trend-why-publishers-consolidating/.

27 Tracy and Lee, "Vox Media Acquires New York Magazine."

28 Kumar and Schenk, "Union Renewal and Organizational Change," 36.

29 Murray, "Union Renewal," 13.

30 Christian Levesque and Gregor Murray, "Understanding Union Power: Resources and Capabilities for Renewing Union Capacity," *Transfer* 16, no. 3 (2010): 343.

31 Fantasia, *Cultures of Solidarity*, 11.

32 Jane McAlevey and Bob Ostertag, *Raising Expectations (and Raising Hell): My Decade Fighting for the Labor Movement* (New York: Verso, 2012), 12.

33 Gindin, in Maisano, "The Crisis in American Labor."

34 Fantasia, *Cultures of Solidarity*, 232–3.

35 Marc Tracy, "How Deadspin Imploded," *New York Times*, October 31, 2019, www.nytimes.com/2019/10/31/business/media/deadspin-was-a-good-website.html.

36 See Megan Greenwell, "The Adults in the Room," *Deadspin*, August 23, 2019, https://theconcourse.deadspin.com/the-adults-in-the-room-1837487584.

37 Fantasia, *Cultures of Solidarity*, 233.

38 Alexia Fernández Campbell, "What the Mass Resignations at Deadspin Tell Us about Work in America," *Vox*, November 1, 2019, www.vox.com/identities/2019/11/1/20941677/deadspin-resignations-writers-workers-quit.

Bibliography

Agreement between Slate Magazine and the Writers Guild of America, East.

Agreement between the Huffington Post and the Writers Guild of America, East.

Alexander, Jeffrey C., Elizabeth Butler Breese, and María Leungo, eds. *The Crisis of Journalism Reconsidered: Democratic Culture, Professional Codes, Digital Future*. New York: Cambridge University Press, 2016.

Banks, Miranda J. "The Picket Line Online: Creative Labor, Digital Activism, and the 2007–2008 Writers Guild of America Strike." *Popular Communication* 8, no. 1 (2010): 20–33.

Barbrook, Richard, and Andy Cameron. "The Californian Ideology." *Mute* 1, no. 3 (1995). www.metamute.org/editorial/articles/californian-ideology.

Bell, Emily, and Taylor Owen. *The Platform Press: How Silicon Valley Reengineered Journalism*. Tow Center for Digital Journalism, Columbia University, March 2017. www.cjr.org/tow_center_reports/platform-press-how-silicon-valley-reengineered-journalism.php.

Bennet, Lance W., and Alexandra Segerberg. "Digital Media and the Personalization of Collective Action." *Information, Communication & Society* 14, no. 6 (2011): 770–99.

Benton, Joshua. "America's Largest Union of Journalists Is Doing a Rewrite of Its Leadership Election." *NiemanLab*, August 14, 2019. www.niemanlab.org/2019/08/americas-largest-union-of-journalists-is-doing-a-rewrite-of-its-leadership-election/.

Brasch, Walter M. *With Just Cause: Unionization of the American Journalist*. Lanham: University Press of America, 1991.

Brennen, Bonnie. "The Emergence of Class Consciousness in the American Newspaper Guild." In *Class and News*, edited by Don Heider, 233–47. Lanham: Rowman & Littlefield, 2004.

Bronfenbrenner, Kate. "The Role of Union Strategies in NLRB Certification Elections." *ILR Review* 50, no. 2 (1997): 195–212.

Bui, Kristina, and Nastaran Mohit. "After 136 Years, L.A. Times Journalists Win Their Union." *Labor Notes*, March 1, 2018. www.labornotes.org/2018/03/after-136-years-la-times-journalists-win-their-union.

Chang, Clio. "How to Save Journalism." *The New Republic*, July 11, 2019. https://newrepublic.com/article/154455/save-journalism.

Christian, Harry. "Journalists' Occupational Ideologies and Press Commercialisation." In *The Sociology of Journalism and the Press*, edited by Harry Christian, 259–306. Sociological Review Monograph 29. Staffordshire: University of
Keele, 1980.

Cohen, Michelle. "Thrillist Co-Founder Ben Lerer Lists Colorful, Pop Art-Filled
Soho Loft for $7.4M." *6SQFT*, February 13, 2017. www.6sqft.com/thrillist-co-
founder-ben-lerer-lists-colorful-pop-art-filled-soho-loft-for-7-4m/.

Cohen, Nicole S. "At Work in the Digital Newsroom." *Digital Journalism* 7, no. 5
(2019): 571–91.

Cohen, Nicole S. *Writers' Rights: Freelance Journalism in a Digital Age*. Montreal
and Kingston: McGill-Queen's University Press, 2016.

Cohen, Nicole S., and Greig de Peuter. "'I Work at VICE Canada and I Need a
Union': Organizing Digital Media." In *Labour under Attack: Anti-Unionism in
Canada*, edited by Stephanie Ross and Larry Savage, 114–28. Halifax and Win-
nipeg: Fernwood, 2018.

Cohen, Nicole S., and Greig de Peuter. "Write, Post, Unionize: Journalists and Self-
Organization." *Notes from Below* 7 (June 8, 2019). https://notesfrombelow.org/
article/write-post-unionize.

*Collective Bargaining Agreement between Portfolio Media, Inc. d/b/a Law360 & The
NewsGuild of New York, Local 31003, CWA*, December 19, 2018–December 31,
2022.

*Collective Bargaining Agreement between Salon Media Group and the Writers
Guild of America, East*, October 12, 2018–December 31, 2021.

*Collective Bargaining Agreement between the Writers Guild of America, East and
First Look Media Works, Inc.*

*Collective Bargaining Agreement, Writers Guild of America, East and Gawker
Media.*

*Collective Bargaining Agreement, Writers Guild of America, East and Thrillist
Media Group, Inc.*, 2018–2021.

*Collective Bargaining Agreement, Writers Guild of America, East and Vice Media,
LLC*, January 1, 2019–December 31, 2021.

Compton, James R., and Paul Benedetti. "Labour, New Media and the Institutional
Restructuring of Journalism." *Journalism Studies* 11, no. 4 (2010): 487–99.

Croucher, Richard, and Geoffrey Wood. "Union Renewal in Historical Perspective."
Work, Employment & Society 31, no. 6 (2017): 1010–20.

Deck, Cecilia. "History of the Newspaper Guild in Canada 1936–1986." In *Essays
in Journalism*, edited by Heather Hiscox, 15–34. London: University of Western
Ontario, 1988.

Deleuze, Gilles. *Spinoza: Practical Philosophy*. San Francisco: City Lights Books,
1998.

DePillis, Lydia. "Why Internet Journalists Don't Unionize." *The Washington Post*,
January 30, 2015. www.washingtonpost.com/news/storyline/wp/2015/01/30/why-
internet-journalists-dont-organize.

Deuze, Mark. "What Is Journalism? Professional Identity and Ideology of Journalists Reconsidered." *Journalism* 6, no. 4 (2005): 443–65.

Doorey, David J. "The Medium and the 'Anti-Union' Message: 'Forced Listening' and Captive Audience Meetings in Canadian Labor Law." *Comparative Labor Law and Policy Journal* 29 (2007): 79–117.

Dundon, Tony, and Gregor Gall. "Anti-Unionism: Contextual and Thematic Issues." In *Global Anti-Unionism: Nature, Dynamics, Trajectories and Outcomes*, edited Gregor Gall and Tony Dundon, 1–17. London: Palgrave Macmillan, 2013.

Eidelson, Josh. "New Yorker Fact-Checkers Win Employee Status after Union Push." *Bloomberg*, September 3, 2019. www.bloomberg.com/news/articles/2019-09-03/new-yorker-fact-checkers-win-employee-status-after-union-push.

Eikhof, Doris Ruth, and Chris Warhurst. "The Promised Land? Why Social Inequalities Are Systemic in the Creative Industries." *Employee Relations* 35, no. 5 (2013): 495–508.

Fantasia, Rick. *Cultures of Solidarity: Consciousness, Action, and Contemporary American Workers*. Berkeley: University of California Press, 1988.

Farbman, Jason. "Organizing New Media." *Jacobin*, November 17, 2016. www.jacobinmag.com/2016/11/gawker-union-gizmodo-deadspin-organized-labor-online-univision-writers-guild/.

Fernández Campbell, Alexia. "What the Mass Resignations at Deadspin Tell Us about Work in America." *Vox*, November 1, 2019. www.vox.com/identities/2019/11/1/20941677/deadspin-resignations-writers-workers-quit.

Fingerhut, Hannah. "More Americans View Long-Term Decline in Union Membership Negatively Than Positively." *Pew Research Center*, June 5, 2018. www.pewresearch.org/fact-tank/2018/06/05/more-americans-view-long-term-decline-in-union-membership-negatively-than-positively/.

Freeman, Richard, and Wayne Diamond. "Young Workers and Trade Unions." In *Representing Workers: Trade Union Recognition and Membership in Britain*, edited by Howard Gospel and Stephen Wood, 29–50. London: Routledge, 2003.

Gahan, Peter, and Andreas Pekarek. "Social Movement Theory, Collective Action Frames and Union Theory: A Critique and Extension." *British Journal of Industrial Relations* 51, no. 4 (2013): 754–76.

Gall, Gregor. "Employer Opposition to Union Recognition." In *Union Organizing: Campaigning for Trade Union Recognition*, edited by Gregor Gall, 79–96. London: Routledge, 2003.

Garst, Aron. "How Video Game Unionization Would Happen." *Variety*, December 17, 2018. https://variety.com/2018/gaming/features/video-game-industry-union-unionization-1203091114/.

Gasher, Mike, Colette Brin, Christine Crowther, Gretchen King, Errol Salamon, and Simon Thibault, eds. *Journalism in Crisis: Bridging Theory and Practice for Democratic Media Strategies in Canada*. Toronto: University of Toronto Press, 2016.

Goggin, Benjamin. "Did Mic Layoff Their Entire Editorial Staff Ahead of Their Sale to Bustle Media Group to Break a Union?" *Business Insider*, December 1, 2018. www.businessinsider.com/mic-layoff-bustle-union-labor.

Greenhouse, Steven. "More Secure Jobs, Bigger Paychecks." *Columbia Journalism Review* (Spring/Summer 2018). www.cjr.org/special_report/media-unions-history.php/.

Greenwell, Megan. "The Adults in the Room." *Deadspin*, August 23, 2019. https:// theconcourse.deadspin.com/the-adults-in-the-room-1837487584.

Gregg, Melissa. "On Friday Night Drinks: Workplace Affects in the Age of the Cubicle." In *The Affect Theory Reader*, edited by Melissa Gregg and Gregory J. Seigworth, 250–68. Durham: Duke University Press, 2010.

Gregg, Melissa. *Work's Intimacy*. Cambridge: Polity, 2011.

Grieco, Elizabeth. "Newsroom Employment Dropped Nearly a Quarter in Less Than 10 Years, with Greatest Decline at Newspapers." *Pew Research Center*, July 30, 2018. www.pewresearch.org/fact-tank/2018/07/30/newsroom-employ ment-dropped-nearly-a-quarter-in-less-than-10-years-with-greatest-decline-at-newspapers/.

Grieco, Elizabeth. "U.S. Newsroom Employment Has Dropped by a Quarter since 2008, with Greatest Decline at Newspapers." *Pew Research Centre*, July 9, 2019. www.pewresearch.org/fact-tank/2019/07/09/u-s-newsroom-employment-has-dropped-by-a-quarter-since-2008/.

Hardt, Hanno, and Bonnie Brennen, eds. *Newsworkers: Toward a History of the Rank and File*. Minneapolis: University of Minnesota Press, 1995.

Hardy, Kate, and Katie Cruz. "Affective Organizing: Collectivizing Informal Sex Workers in an Intimate Union." *American Behavioral Scientist* 63, no. 2 (2019): 244–61.

Harris, Elizabeth A., and Robin Pogrebin. "Inside Hushed Museum Hallways, a Rumble over Low Pay Grows Louder." *New York Times*, July 22, 2019. www. nytimes.com/2019/07/22/arts/museum-pay-unions.html.

Haynes, Peter, Jack Vowles, and Peter Boxall. "Explaining the Younger-Older Worker Union Density Gap." *British Journal of Industrial Relations* 43, no. 1 (2005): 93–116.

Hennessy, Rosemary. "Open Secrets: The Affective Cultures of Organizing on Mexico's Northern Border." *Feminist Theory* 10, no. 3 (2009): 309–22.

Henwood, Doug. "Unions Still Haven't Rebounded." *Jacobin*, January 25, 2019. www.jacobinmag.com/2019/01/union-density-united-states-2018-bls.

Hesmondhalgh, David. *The Cultural Industries*, 3rd Edition. London: Sage, 2013.

Heyward, Anna. "The Story behind the Unjust Shutdown of Gothamist and DNAinfo." *The New Yorker*, November 14, 2017. www.newyorker.com/culture/culture-desk/the-story-behind-the-unjust-shutdown-of-gothamist-and-dnainfo.

Heywood, Broun. *It Seems to Me, 1925–1935*. New York: Harcourt, Brace and Company, 1935.

Hirschman, Albert O. *Exit, Voice, and Loyalty: Responses to Decline in Firms, Organizations, and States*. Cambridge: Harvard University Press, 1970.

Hodder, Andy, and Lefteris Krestos. "Young Workers and Unions: Context and Overview." In *Young Workers and Trade Unions: A Global View*, edited by Andy Hodder and Lefteris Krestos, 1–15. New York: Palgrave Macmillan, 2015.

Holgate, Jane, Melanie Simms, and Maite Tapia. "The Limitations of the Theory and Practice of Mobilization in Trade Union Organizing." *Economic and Industrial Democracy* 39, no. 4 (2018): 599–616.

Jaffe, Sarah. "A Group of Workers Corporate America Claimed Were Impossible to Organize Win Key Union Votes." *AlterNet*, January 10, 2011. www.alternet.

org/economy/149476/a_group_of_workers_corporate_america_claimed_were_
impossible_to_organize_win_key_union_votes/.

James, Meg. "Los Angeles Times Reaches Historic Agreement with Its News-room." *Lost Angeles Times*, October 16, 2019. www.latimes.com/california/story/2019-10-16/los-angeles-times-first-guild-contract.

Jerde, Sara. "Media Mergers Aren't New: So Why Are Publishers Consolidating Now?" *Adweek*, October 14, 2019. www.adweek.com/digital/media-mergers-trend-why-publishers-consolidating/.

Juravich, Tom, Kate Bronfenbrenner, and Robert Hickey. "Significant Victories: An Analysis of Union First Contracts." In *Justice on the Job: Perspectives on the Erosion of Collective Bargaining in the United States*, edited by Richard N. Block, Sheldon Friedman, Michelle Kaminski, and Andy Levin, 87–114. Kalamazoo: W.E. Upjohn Institute for Employment Research, 2006.

Kelly, John. *Rethinking Industrial Relations: Mobilization, Collectivism and Long Waves*. London and New York: Routledge, 1998.

Kelly, John, and Vidu Badigannavar. "Union Organizing." In *Union Organizing and Activity*, edited by John E. Kelly and Paul Willman, 32–50. London: Routledge, 2004.

Kelly, Keith J. "Tronc Is Looking for New Head of Labor Relations." *New York Post*, September 18, 2018. https://nypost.com/2018/09/18/tronc-looking-for-new-head-of-labor-relations/.

Kelly, Kim. "Seize the Media." *Commune*, May 2, 2019. https://communemag.com/seize-the-media/.

Kim, E. Tammy. "Unionizing the Digital Newsroom." *Dissent*, July 19, 2016. www.dissentmagazine.org/online_articles/unionizing-digital-newsroom.

Klare, Karl E. "Labor Law as Ideology: Toward a New Historiography of Collective Bargaining Law." *Industrial Relations Law Journal* 4, no. 3 (1981): 450–82.

Kolins Givan, Rebecca, and Lena Hipp. "Public Perceptions of Union Efficacy: A Twenty-Four Country Study." *Labor Studies Journal* 37, no. 1 (2012): 7–32.

Kumar, Pradeep, and Christopher Schenk. "Union Renewal and Organizational Change: A Review of the Literature." In *Paths to Union Renewal: The Canadian Experience*, edited by Pradeep Kumar and Christopher Schenk, 29–60. Guelph: Broadview Press, 2006.

Labor Video Project. "Democracy Depends on Journalism, Journalism Depends on the Union: Digital Media Workers Speak Out." *Panel at Labor Notes Conference*, Chicago, April 17, 2018. www.youtube.com/watch?v=wAaoIjjPRto.

Lasarow, Bill. "AOL-Huffington Post: The Virtual Picket Line." *The Guardian*, March 28, 2011. www.theguardian.com/commentisfree/cifamerica/2011/mar/28/huffington-post-aol.

L.A. Times Guild. "Contract Summary and Highlights." 2019. Accessed October 18, 2019. https://static1.squarespace.com/static/59f32b4b12abd94fac1a508b/t/5d a7c1c24e131701f4efb48b/1571275203091/Contract+Summary+%281%29.pdf.

L.A. Times Guild. "L.A. Times Guild Reaches Agreement with Management on Historic First Contract." *LA Times Guild*, October 16, 2019. https://latguild.com/news/2019/10/16/los-angeles-times-guild-reaches-agreement.

Law360 Guild. "The Union Busting Playbook." Accessed October 9, 2019. www.law360guild.org/union-busting.

Leab, Daniel J. *A Union of Individuals: The Formation of the American Newspaper Guild, 1933–1936*. New York: Columbia University Press, 1970.

Lee, Jacquie. "Union Activists Take Notice of Workers' Twitter Savvy." *Bloomberg Law*, January 30, 2018. https://news.bloomberglaw.com/daily-labor-report/union-activists-take-notice-of-workers-twitter-savvy.

Legault, Marie-Josée, and Johanna Weststar. "The Capacity for Mobilization in Project-Based Cultural Work: A Case of the Video Game Industry." *Canadian Journal of Communication* 49 (2015): 203–21.

Lepie, Jonathan. "Is There a Winning Formula for Union Organizing?" *Employee Rights and Responsibilities Journal* 26, no. 2 (2014): 137–52.

Levesque, Christian, and Gregor Murray. "Understanding Union Power: Resources and Capabilities for Renewing Union Capacity." *Transfer* 16, no. 3 (2010): 333–50.

Lewis, Cora. "BuzzFeed Founder Jonah Peretti: 'I Don't Think a Union Is Right' for Staff." *BuzzFeed*, August 14, 2015. www.buzzfeednews.com/article/coralewis/buzzfeed-founder-jonah-peretti-i-dont-think-a-union-is-right.

Lopez, German. "I Was Skeptical of Unions: Then I Joined One." *Vox*, August 19, 2019. www.vox.com/policy-and-politics/2019/8/19/20727283/unions-good-income-inequality-wealth.

Maisano, Chris. "The Crisis in American Labor: An Interview with Sam Gindin." *Jacobin*, January 8, 2019. https://jacobinmag.com/2013/02/sam-gindin-on-the-crisis-in-american-labor/.

Marans, Daniel. "Fusion Staff Pressures CEO for Union Recognition." *HuffPost US*, October 24, 2016. www.huffingtonpost.ca/entry/fusion-staff-pressure-ceo-for-union-recognition_n_580e69c2e4b02444efa4c7db.

Markowitz, Linda. "After the Organizing Ends: Workers, Self-Efficacy, Activism, and Union Frameworks." *Social Problems* 45, no. 3 (1998): 356–82.

Martin, Christopher R. *Framed! Labor and the Corporate Media*. Ithaca: Cornell University Press, 2004.

Massumi, Brian. *Politics of Affect*. Cambridge: Polity, 2015.

McAlevey, Jane. *No Shortcuts: Organizing for Power in the New Gilded Age*. Oxford: Oxford University Press, 2016.

McAlevey, Jane, and Bob Ostertag. *Raising Expectations (and Raising Hell): My Decade Fighting for the Labor Movement*. New York: Verso, 2012.

McChesney, Robert W., and Victor Pickard, eds. *Will the Last Reporter Please Turn Out the Lights: The Collapse of Journalism and What Can Be Done to Fix It*. New York: The New Press, 2011.

McCormick, Andrew. "A Law Firm in the Trenches against Media Unions." *Columbia Journalism Review*, December 13, 2018. www.cjr.org/analysis/jones-day-unions-slate-strike.php.

McKercher, Catherine. *Newsworkers Unite: Labor, Convergence, and North American Newspapers*. Lanham: Rowman & Littlefield, 2002.

Mic Union. "From Mic Union to Media Management: We Are Watching." *The NewsGuild of New York*, January 18, 2019. www.nyguild.org/front-page-details/from-mic-union-resolutions-for-digital-media.

Moore, Phoebe. "Tracking Affective Labour for Agility in the Quantified Workplace." *Body & Society* 24, no. 3 (2018): 39–67.

The MTV News Unionizing Committee. "Why We're Organizing." *Writers Guild of America, East*. Accessed October 9, 2019. digitalwritersunion.org/mtv.

Murphy, Caroline. "Fear and Leadership in Union Organizing Campaigns: An Examination of Workplace Activist Behavior." *Journal of Workplace Rights* (January–March 2016). https://doi.org/10.1177/2158244015623932.

Murray, Gregor. "Union Renewal: What Can We Learn from Three Decades of Research?" *Transfer* 23, no. 1 (2017): 9–29.

National Writers Union. "Freelance Solidarity Project." *National Writers Union*. Accessed October 15, 2019. https://nwu.org/freelance-solidarity-project/.

Neilson, Tai. "Unions in Digital Labour Studies: A Review of Information Society and Marxist Autonomist Approaches." *tripleC* 16, no. 2 (2018): 882–900.

Newman, Andy. "Gothamist and DNAinfo Newsrooms Now Have a Union." *The New York Times*, October 27, 2017. www.nytimes.com/2017/10/27/nyregion/dnainfo-gothamist-union.html.

The New Republic. "The New Republic's Leadership Advances Proposal for Unionization of All Staff." *The New Republic*, April 18, 2018. https://newrepublic.com/article/148041/new-republics-leadership-advances-proposal-unionization-staff.

The NewsGuild of New York, Local 310003, CWA. "Law360 Union Members Secure Progressive, Strong First Contract." December 18, 2018. www.nyguild.org/post/law360-union-members-secure-progressive-strong-first-contract.

News Media Guild: Guardian US Collective Bargaining Agreement, 2017–2020.

Newspaper Guild of New York. "Guild Negotiates First Contract at Times Company Digital." December 13, 1999. https://web.archive.org/web/20001206134000/www.nyguild.org/loc006.htm.

Nolan, Hamilton. "The Dismal Thrillist Anti-Union Campaign." *The Concourse*, October 3, 2017. https://theconcourse.deadspin.com/the-dismal-thrillist-anti-union-campaign-1793157413.

Nolan, Hamilton. "Here Is Vice Media's Salary Breakdown." *Gawker*, December 18, 2014. http://gawker.com/here-is-vice-medias-salary-breakdown-1672760767.

Nolan, Hamilton. "New York Magazine Hosts Union-Busting Meeting." *Splinter*, September 6, 2018. https://splinternews.com/new-york-magazine-hosts-union-busting-meeting-1828841682.

Nolan, Hamilton. "The Single Most Insufferable Response to Our Vice Media Story." *Gawker*, June 2, 2014. http://gawker.com/the-single-most-insufferable-response-to-our-vice-media-1584736050.

Nolan, Hamilton. "StoryCorps, of All Places, Is Running an Anti-Union Campaign." *Splinter*, June 27, 2017. https://splinternews.com/storycorps-of-all-places-is-running-an-anti-union-cam-1796429329.

Nolan, Hamilton. "Why We've Decided to Organize." *Gawker*, April 16, 2015. https://gawker.com/why-weve-decided-to-organize-1698246231.

Nolan, Hamilton. "Working at Vice Media Is Not as Cool as It Seems." *Gawker*, May 30, 2014. http://gawker.com/working-at-vice-media-is-not-as-cool-as-it-seems-1579711577.

Örnebring, Henrik. "Technology and Journalism-as-Labour: Historical Perspectives." *Journalism* 11, no. 1 (2010): 57–74.

Osberg, Molly. "BuzzFeed London: Layoffs Coming, Unions Busten, Christmas Cancelled, But Free Caviar." *Splinter*, December 22, 2017. https://splinternews.com/buzzfeed-london-layoffs-coming-unions-busted-christm-1821532976.

Petre, Caitlin. "Engineering Consent: How the Design and Marketing of Newsroom Analytics Tools Rationalized Journalists' Labor." *Digital Journalism* 6, no. 4 (2018): 509–27.

Pickard, Victor. "The Violence of the Market." *Journalism* 20, no. 1 (2019): 154–8.

Prasad, Revati. "An Organized Workforce Is Part of Growing Up: Gawker and the Case for Unionizing Digital Newsrooms." *Communication, Culture & Critique* (March 2019). https://doi.org/10.1093/ccc/tcz008.

Press, Alex. "I've Got Your Back, and You've Got Mine." *Jacobin*, October 28, 2017. www.jacobinmag.com/2017/10/los-angeles-times-union-organizing.

Proffitt, Jennifer M. "Solidarity in the Newsroom? Media Concentration and Union Organizing: A Case Study from the Sunshine State." *Journalism* (June 2019). https://doi.org/10.1177/1464884919860030.

Puette, William. *Through Jaundiced Eyes: How the Media View Organized Labour.* Ithaca: Cornell University Press, 1992.

Rhomberg, Chris. *The Broken Table: The Detroit Newspaper Strike and the State of American Labor.* New York: Russell Sage Foundation, 2012.

Rollman, Hans. "Should Unions Say No to Closed-Door Negotiations?" *Briarpatch*, June 28, 2018. https://briarpatchmagazine.com/articles/view/should-unions-say-no-to-closed-door-negotiations.

Ross, Stephanie. "Varieties of Social Unionism: Towards a Framework for Comparison." *Just Labour: A Canadian Journal of Work and Society* 11 (2007): 16–34.

Ross, Stephanie, and Larry Savage. "An Introduction to Anti-Unionism in Canada." In *Labour under Attack: Anti-Unionism in Canada*, edited by Stephanie Ross and Larry Savage, 3–18. Halifax and Winnipeg: Fernwood, 2018.

Russell-Kraft, Stephanie. "The Aggressive Anti-Union Campaign at StoryCorps." *The Nation*, July 17, 2017. www.thenation.com/article/the-aggressive-anti-union-campaign-at-storycorps/.

Saha, Anamik. *Race and the Cultural Industries.* Cambridge: Polity Press, 2018.

Salamon, Errol. "Digital Media Workers Are Unionizing Like It's 1999." *CMG Freelance*, March 23, 2016. http://cmgfreelance.ca/en/digital-media-workers-are-unionizing-like-its-1999/.

Salamon, Errol. "Digitizing Freelance Media Labor: A Class of Workers Negotiates Entrepreneurialism and Activism." *New Media & Society* (July 2019). https://doi.org/10.1177/1461444819861958.

Sangster, Jane. "The Softball Solution: Female Workers, Male Managers, and the Operation of Paternalism at Westclox, 1923–60." *Labour/Le Travail* 32 (1993): 167–99.

Schleuss, Jon. "Jon's Platform." Accessed October 15, 2019. www.jonforpresident.com/platform.

Schoeneborn, Dennis, Timothy R. Kuhn, and Dan Kärreman. "The Communicative Constitution of Organization, Organizing, and Organizationality." *Organization Studies* 40, no. 4 (2019): 475–96.

Seigworth, Gregory J., and Melissa Gregg. "An Inventory of Shimmers." In *The Affect Theory Reader*, edited by Melissa Gregg and Gregory J. Seigworth, 1–25. Durham: Duke University Press, 2010.

Sherwood, Merryn, and Penny O'Donnell. "Once a Journalist, Always a Journalist? Industry Restructure, Job Loss and Professional Identity." *Journalism Studies* 19, no. 7 (2016): 1021–38.

Siegelbaum, Sasu, and Ryan J. Thomas. "Putting the Work (Back) Into Newswork: Searching for the Sources of Normative Failure." *Journalism Practice* 10, no. 3 (2016): 387–404.

Silver, Beverly J. *Forces of Labor: Workers' Movements and Globalization since 1870*. Cambridge: Cambridge University Press, 2003.

Simms, Melanie, and Jane Holgate. "Organising for What? Where Is the Debate on the Politics of Organising?" *Work, Employment and Society* 24, no. 1 (2010): 157–68.

Slinn, Sara. "Captive Audience Meetings and Forced Listening: Lessons for Canada from the American Experience." *Relations Industrielles/Industrial Relations* 63, no. 4 (2008): 694–718.

Solomon, William S. "The Site of Newsroom Labor: The Division of Editorial Practices." In *Newsworkers: Toward a History of the Rank and File*, edited by Hanno Hardt and Bonnie Brennen, 110–34. Minneapolis: University of Minnesota Press, 1995.

Statistics Canada. "5123–Journalists." *National Occupational Classification 2011*, 2018. Accessed October 16, 2019. http://www23.statcan.gc.ca/imdb/p3VD.pl?Function=getVD&TVD=122372&CVD=122376&CPV=5123&CST=01012011&CLV=4&MLV=4.

Steel, Emily. "At Vice, Cutting-Edge Media and Old-School Allegations of Sexual Harassment." *New York Times*, December 23, 2017. www.nytimes.com/2017/12/23/business/media/vice-sexual-harassment.html.

Sterne, Peter. "News Guild Starts $500,000 Campaign to Organize Digital Newsrooms." *Politico*, September 1, 2015. www.politico.com/media/story/2015/09/news-guild-starts-500-000-campaign-to-organize-digital-newsrooms-004198.

Sterne, Peter. "Nick Denton 'Intensely Relaxed' by Gawker's Union Drive." *Politico*, April 16, 2015. www.politico.com/media/story/2015/04/nick-denton-intensely-relaxed-by-gawkers-union-drive-003863.

Stone, Madeline. "VICE CEO Shane Smith Bought a Mansion in Santa Monica for $23 Million." *Business Insider*, August 10, 2015. www.businessinsider.com/vice-ceo-shane-smith-buys-santa-monica-mansion-for-23-million-2015-8.

Strachan, Maxwell. "The Fall of Mic Was a Warning." *HuffPost US*, July 23, 2019. www.huffingtonpost.ca/entry/mic-layoffs-millennial-digital-news-site-warning_n_5c8c144fe4b03e83bdc0e0bc.

Szeman, Imre. "Entrepreneurship as the New Common Sense." *The South Atlantic Quarterly* 114, no. 3 (July 2015): 471–90.

Tani, Maxwell. "Hearst Magazine Staffers Unionizing across Two Dozen Publications, Forming Giant for Writers Guild of America." *The Daily Beast*, November 11, 2019. www.thedailybeast.com/hearst-magazines-staffers-are-unionizing-across-two-dozen-publications-joining-writers-guild-of-america-east.

Tani, Maxwell. "Vox Employees Are Going on a 'Slack Strike' to Push for a Union." *Business Insider*, January 3, 2018. www.businessinsider.com/vox-employees-are-going-on-a-slack-strike-to-push-for-a-union-2018-1.

Tarrow, Sidney. "Mentalities, Political Cultures, and Collective Action Frames: Constructing Meanings through Action." In *Frontiers in Social Movement Theory*, edited by Aldon D. Morris and Carol McClurg Mueller, 174–202. New Haven: Yale University Press, 1992.

Taylor, Astra. "Against Activism." *The Baffler*, no. 30 (2016). https://thebaffler.com/salvos/against-activism.

Tracy, Marc. "How Deadspin Imploded." *New York Times*, October 31, 2019. www.nytimes.com/2019/10/31/business/media/deadspin-was-a-good-website.html.

Tracy, Marc, and Edmund Lee. "Vox Media Acquires New York Magazine, Chronicler of the Highbrow and Lowbrow." *The New York Times*, September 24, 2019. www.nytimes.com/2019/09/24/business/media/vox-buys-nymag.html.

Uberti, David. "Slate's Biggest Enemies Are Donald Trump and Its Staff Trying to Unionize." *Splinter*, March 8, 2017. https://splinternews.com/slates-biggest-enemies-are-donald-trump-and-its-staff-t-1797446734.

Uetricht, Micah, and Barry Eidlin. "U.S. Union Revitalization and the Missing 'Militant Minority'." *Labor Studies Journal* 44, no. 1 (2019): 36–59.

Waterson, Jim. "BuzzFeed UK Staff Reject Chance to Unionize." *The Guardian*, July 18, 2018. www.theguardian.com/media/2018/jul/18/buzzfeed-uk-staff-reject-chance-to-join-nuj.

Watson, H.G. "No Union at National Post after CWA Canada Loses Certification Vote." *J-Source*, April 27, 2018. https://j-source.ca/article/no-union-at-national-post-after-cwa-canada-loses-certification-vote/.

Wells, Richard. "Connecting the Dots: Labor and the Digital Landscape." *Labor Studies in Working-Class History* 15, no. 3 (2018): 55–76.

Wiedeman, Reeves. "A Company Built on a Bluff." *New York*, June 10, 2018. http://nymag.com/daily/intelligencer/2018/06/inside-vice-media-shane-smith.html.

Williams, Raymond. *Culture and Materialism: Selected Essays*. London: Verso, 1980.

Winant, Gabriel. "Who Works for the Workers?" *N+1* 26 (Fall 2016). https://nplusonemag.com/issue-26/essays/who-works-for-the-workers/.

Windham, Lane. "This Is Your Daughter's Labor Movement." *Portside*, June 28, 2018. https://portside.org/2018-06-28/your-daughters-labor-movement.

Wong, Julia Carrie. "Google Staff Condemn Treatment of Temp Workers in 'Historic' Show of Solidarity." *The Guardian*, April 2, 2019. www.theguardian.com/technology/2019/apr/02/google-workers-sign-letter-temp-contractors-protest.

Writers Guild of America, East. "Vox Media Ratifies Landmark First Contract with Writers Guild of America, East." *WGAE, Press Room*, June 14, 2019. www.wgaeast.org/vox-media-ratifies-landmark-first-contract-with-writers-guild-of-america-east/.

Yates, Charlotte. "The Road to Union Renewal: From Organizing the Unorganized to New Political Alternatives." *Canadian Dimension*, March 1, 2004. https://canadiandimension.com/articles/view/the-road-to-union-renewal-from-organizing-the-unorganized-to-new-political.

Yelland, Tannara. Presentation at "Remaking Game Work," public forum, Toronto Media Arts Centre, July 17, 2019.

Index

Printed in the United States
by Baker & Taylor Publisher Services